# WHAT IS

# GOD

# REALLY LIKE?

# WHAT IS

# GOD

## REALLY LIKE?

CRAIG GROESCHEL

GENERAL EDITOR

ZONDERVAN®

ZONDERVAN.com/
AUTHORTRACKER
*follow your favorite authors*

ZONDERVAN

*What Is God Really Like?*
Copyright © 2010 by Craig Groeschel

This title is also available as a Zondervan ebook. Visit www.zondervan.com/ebooks.

This title is also available in a Zondervan audio edition. Visit www.zondervan.fm.

Requests for information should be addressed to:

Zondervan, *Grand Rapids, Michigan 49530*

Library of Congress Cataloging-in-Publication Data

What is God really like? / Craig Groeschel, general editor.
    p. cm.
    ISBN 978-0-310-32833-9 (hardcover, jacketed)  1.  God (Christianity)  I. Groeschel, Craig.
BT103.W48 2010
    231'.4—dc22                                                                              2010003539

Craig Groeschel is represented by Thomas J. Winters of Winters & King, Inc., Tulsa, Oklahoma.

Cover design: *John Hamilton Design*
Interior design: *Matthew VanZomeren*

*Printed in the United States of America*

10  11  12  13  14  15  /DCI/  23  22  21  20  19  18  17  16  15  14  13  12  11  10  9  8  7  6  5  4  3  2  1

# CONTENTS

# INTRODUCTION
# GOD IS ...

*Craig Groeschel*

One afternoon several years ago, my doorbell rang. I answered, politely acknowledging the twenty-something-year-old guy smiling warmly on my doorstep.

"Can I help you?" I asked.

Almost immediately, he began sharing his faith in Christ with me. Now, not only am I a Christian, but I'm also a pastor. But he was doing so well, his passion so genuine, his smile so infectious, that I just couldn't bring myself to stop him. He looked like he had just won the lottery. After thirty seconds or so, I realized I shouldn't waste his time, and I needed to come (mostly) clean:

"Man, I'm *so* glad you're out witnessing about Christ," I said sincerely. "I think I should probably let you know, though ... I'm actually already a committed believer."

"That's awesome!" he half-shouted, his eyes shining. "You've *gotta* come with me to my church. Seriously, it's the best church in town!"

So I told him I'm already part of a church.

"That's great, man!" he said enthusiastically. "What church do you go to?"

"It's called Life Church."

His countenance dropped from lottery winner to food-poisoning victim. He drew in a deep breath and regained in his composure. Glancing around, he leaned in and half-whispered, "Dude, I hate to say it, but you probably shouldn't go to Life Church. My pastor says your pastor doesn't preach the truth."

Now I had to practice composure. I almost said, "Yeah? Well, you can tell *your* pastor that the pastor of Life Church wants to meet him in a dark alley and introduce him to the truth!"

Instead, I smiled weakly and said, "Well, thanks for coming, man. I have to go now. May the Lord bless you, okay?"

## MAY THEY BE ONE

According to the *World Christian Encyclopedia* (Oxford Univ. Press, 2001), the Christian faith has some 33,830 denominations. That's an awful lot of diversity! On the one hand, with that many approaches, there should be something for everyone. On the other hand, it's possible the word *denomination* might actually break God's heart. The Latin origin of *de-* means "apart," while *nominare* means "to name." *Denomination* literally means "to separate by naming." As far as I can tell from the Scriptures, only one name should matter: Jesus.

In John 17:20–23, Jesus prayed an amazing prayer for his disciples ... and for us: "My prayer is not for them alone. I pray also for those who will believe in me through their message, that all of them may be one, Father, just as you are in me and I am in you. May they also be in us so that the world may believe that you have sent me. I have given them the glory that you gave me, that they may be one as we are one: I in them and you in me. May they be brought to complete unity to let the world know that you sent me and have loved them even as you have loved me."

One day as I was visiting with some pastor friends, the question came up, "What if we could be a part of the answer to Jesus' prayer?" Later, when I returned to the church office, the implications of that idea haunted me. What would happen if—for just one month— churches around the world partnered together? What would happen if we fasted and prayed together? What would happen if we all served our communities at the same time in the name of Christ?

What if we all gave generously to start new churches? What would God do if a few of us acted like we were one?

That question eventually gave birth to One Prayer (*www.One-Prayer.com*). In the spring of 2008, I posted an invitation on our blog, *Swerve.lifechurch.tv*, asking churches if they would be willing to partner during the month of June. I sincerely hoped that at least a handful would reply. We were shocked when hundreds of churches from around the world enthusiastically responded. In 2009, we invited churches to work together again. This time, more than two thousand churches, from thirty-nine countries around the world, came together to make a difference in our world.

Different styles of worship. Different backgrounds. Different mission fields. Different ministry philosophies. Yet all share just one Lord and one Savior, Jesus Christ. Together these churches raised enough money to start more than sixteen hundred new churches, in places like India, China, Cambodia, and Sudan.

In John 13:34–35, Jesus tells us the one way that the world will know that we follow him: "A new command I give you: Love one another. As I have loved you, so you must love one another. By this all men will know that you are my disciples, if you love one another." Churches used to be known for their traditions, their buildings, and their style of music. Sadly, in more recent years Christians have become known more for what we're against. Through One Prayer, we're becoming known for our love again.

## GOD IS

The theme for One Prayer 2009 was "God is ..." Pastors from all around the world submitted their messages describing different attributes of God found in the Bible. In uncertain times, God is certain. God is strong—so why aren't his children? God is here, and anything can happen. God is able to overcome the strongholds in our lives. God is merciful, and he wants to give people a fresh start. And those are just a few.

None of the pastors who participated in One Prayer 2009 will profit financially. Together we participated simply because we believe in the unity that One Prayer represents. When God's people act in unity, we see his power to change lives. Any and all royalties generated from every part of One Prayer will be used to plant churches around the world. We hope that learning who God is—through what his Scriptures have to teach us—will lead people to want to know God, and not be satisfied just to know about him. Jesus Christ died for us and for the world. Jesus is the hope of the world, and we are his body, commissioned to bring that hope to them. Each one of us is just one small part.

In the hockey movie *Miracle*, Coach Herb Brooks told his players, "When you pull on that jersey, the name on the front is a lot more important than the one on the back." We don't play for the name on the back: First United Methodist, Peace Lutheran, Resurrection Assembly of God, Holy Ghost Temple of Praise Cathedral of Power and Anointing, or GracePointeLifeTruthHouseRiverNorth.

We're playing for the name of Jesus.

CHAPTER 1

# G O D

## IS STRONG

*Francis Chan*

This one guy in my church is—literally—the strongest man on earth. I'm not exaggerating. He's actually appeared on ESPN. He bench presses something like 1,050 pounds. To baptize him, we had to turn him sideways because our baptismal couldn't hold him. He's huge, the kind of guy whose head extends straight up out of his torso, no neck.

His wife could beat me up. She bench presses over four hundred pounds. (I don't know if you know, but that's a lot for a girl.) I haven't met their children, but I'll bet they're pretty big. It would be really strange if they had scrawny little kids. That wouldn't make any sense.

We serve an all-powerful, amazing, strong God. But we don't focus enough on that aspect of him. Consequently, our churches are filled with people who are scared and weak. It doesn't look right for such a powerful God to have such weak children. *Powerful* is not an adjective I would use to describe most of the people filling churches today. We should talk about the strength of God. God is strong.

How many people would you describe as powerful? Probably not many. I think it's because we believers seldom think about this characteristic of God, so we become weak ourselves. The more I focus on God's strength and power, the more I find I have the courage to do and to say the things that he wants me to.

Those of us who grew up in church learned all the powerful Bible stories. As a kid, I went to Sunday school here and there, and I always looked forward to hearing about David and Goliath. I loved the way that this scrawny little guy called out Goliath: "By the power of my God, where is this uncircumcised Philistine?" I loved this guy who used God's power to take a giant down.

Strength has characterized the followers of God ever since the beginning of time. Remember the story of Shadrach, Meshach, and Abednego? They said, "Go ahead, throw us in a fiery furnace. We're not afraid. We don't care. Our God can deliver us."

Daniel's God was powerful. He said, "Go ahead, throw me in a lion's den. What are lions going to do to me? I have God's strength. He's with me."

Elijah stood on Mount Carmel, facing off against 450 prophets of Baal. As they all danced around and screamed to their god, Elijah just mocked them. He knew what his God was about to do. When they finally finished, he got on his knees and showed them the power of God.

Caleb's story is one of my personal favorites. Caleb and Joshua were two of the twelve spies who went out to spy out Canaan. The spies went, and they realized, "Wow. These people are huge. They're massive. We can't conquer them."

But Caleb said, "Let me at them. Let's go. We can do this thing. God's on our side." He demonstrated power and confidence. Joshua was the same way: "Caleb's right. With God with us, we can conquer any people. It doesn't matter how big they are." The other ten spies and the rest of the people were the cowards. But the believers were always distinguished by their power.

I also love that forty-five years later, in Joshua 14, when they were about to go into battle, eighty-five-year-old Caleb was saying, "I know it has been forty-five years. I know I'm old. But I'm just as strong as I used to be. Let me at them." Caleb was ready to just take charge. He was ready to do the same thing he would have done forty-five years earlier, because he never stopped believing in his God.

I can't help wondering, Where are the eighty-five-year-olds today who think that way? Where are the forty-year-olds who are living with that type of confidence, boldness, and strength? We should evaluate ourselves. In 2 Timothy 1:7, Paul tells Timothy, "For God gave us a spirit not of fear but of power and love and self-control."

A few months ago, I was doing one of those sermons where I try to teach through the whole Bible on one Sunday. (I skipped some things, but I wanted to get through the whole story.) I was making some of it up as I went along, because I've read this thing before. In Revelation, I was reading how great it is for those who conquer. Suddenly in Revelation 21, the conviction hit, because those who wouldn't back down to the mark of the beast said, "No! I'm not taking that mark. You can torture me, starve me to death. I'm not taking it." The end of Revelation 21:7 says, "The one who conquers will have this heritage, and I will be his God and he will be my son."

Then verse 8 says, "But as for the cowardly, the faithless, the detestable, as for murderers, the sexually immoral, sorcerers, idolaters, and all liars, their portion will be in the lake that burns with fire and sulfur, which is the second death." As I was reading, it dawned on me: the first people on that list are cowards. Cowards? I can think of so many times when I was scared—when I knew God wanted me to say something and I didn't, when I knew he wanted me to talk to someone and I didn't. Sometimes in my prayer time with God, I'll read his Word and think, *This says what it says. I just have to go for it. I have to do it.* But then I'll let people talk me out of it. Or I'll talk myself out of it. There are so many things I feel I should do, but then I just walk away.

And yet, when I read this passage about these conquerors, I realize that's what believers, followers of God, should be known for. We should be strong because our God is strong. But we're not known for that. Often, we're scared; we're cowards. It doesn't make sense. If that huge couple had scrawny kids, it would just be weird. In the same way, the Bible portrays followers of this mighty, all-powerful God as fearless conquerors. Winners. The other side—without the Spirit of God—were cowards. Do people see you as powerful? If someone were to describe you, is that a word they would use? Do you have that kind of confidence in your God? Are you *that* sure of what he's able to do through you?

The pastor in me gets so concerned because we have people in our church who supposedly have the Spirit of the living God—the same one who raised Christ from the dead—living in them. We have more resources and more education than any generation before us. Through podcasts, we have every sermon, every commentary, at our fingertips. We have every tool we could possibly need, and yet we say, "I can't go talk to my neighbor. That would be weird."

In Scripture, I read about David going after Goliath. Joshua and Caleb. Elijah. Paul. Peter. Uneducated fishermen took on the whole world. We have so much given to us, and we're like, "What? Walk across the street and start a relationship with them? Tell them about Jesus? That's too much. Maybe I'll bring them to church, where someone else can tell them about Jesus." People can be Christians for decades and still feel unequipped to disciple others. They're afraid to tell someone, "Follow my example, even as I follow Christ's." And yet that's precisely what Jesus told us he wants us to do. Couples who have been married for fifteen, twenty, thirty years say, "Oh, I don't know if I could do premarital counseling. A guy in my church has a PhD in Biblical Counseling. He should do it." How could what we have still not be enough? Years of experience and the Holy Spirit, plus every sermon in the world at our fingertips?

I believe we're simply scared—myself included. What's crazy is that it seems like the longer I'm in church settings, the more scared I become. I think it's because we meet people who are so gifted, and we think, *He's so good; I could never do it like him.* Rather than looking to God's Holy Spirit for inspiration, we instead compare ourselves with others. David could have said, "Those guys are so much bigger than I am." Everyone in Scripture could have done that. We need to remember who we worship. God is the Creator, and he's on our side.

I was playing golf with a buddy of mine, and we joined up with this other twosome. These guys were really good. They parred the first two holes. (I don't do that.) On the next hole, a par three, one of these guys hit it into the sand. I remember thinking, *Oh, good.*

*He made a mistake. Now I'm not so embarrassed.* Then he chipped it out of the sand — into the hole, for a birdie.

I stood there for a second, dumbfounded. Then I said, "Okay, what's going on? I've played with good guys. But you guys are *really* good."

He kind of chuckled. "Yeah, I was on the tour for a while. Like, seven, eight years."

I knew I couldn't beat him because he'd been a tour player, so I figured I'd just outdrive him instead. Because that's what matters. I'd swing as hard as I could, and after a while, I finally started out-driving him on a few holes. As we were nearing the end, I was out-driving him by twenty or thirty yards. (Sure, he was seventy-three years old, but he still hit it far.)

Of course we visited as we played, and I tried sharing my faith with him. I figured, he's seventy-three; I have to share with him. What if he doesn't make it to the end of this hole? I didn't want that on my conscience.

I asked, "So, do you believe in God?"

He glared at me, kind of awkwardly. He said, "You don't bring up God. You don't bring up religion. Don't bring up politics, and don't bring up religion. Don't you know that?"

I didn't.

I'm glad I asked anyway, because apparently making him mad threw off his game. Then I couldn't let it go. Not because it was affecting his game but because, "So you *don't* believe in God?"

He just stood there, staring me down.

I said, "No, honestly, I want to know. I mean, if you don't believe, then where did all *this* come from?" I gestured around us.

He said, "What are you talking about?"

I said, "You know. The trees, the grass."

"Gardeners," he answered curtly.

But I'm stubborn. "You know what I mean: this whole world. Seriously. Like, there was nothing, and then *boom*! All of this is here?"

He said, "Fine. Maybe there's a Creator."

That satisfied me ... for a few minutes.

We played a few more holes and I said, "So, what do you think about the Bible?"

He smirked. "You actually believe in the Bible? That thing's so full of contradictions."

I said, "Tell me one."

He thought for a few seconds. "Okay. Do you *really* believe in Noah's ark? You honestly believe Noah got two camels to walk onto the ark, then two cows behind them, and two little ants? Did he talk to the ants?" He mocked, like he was Noah saying it: "Come on, little ants!"

I can't report that I had great success with this guy, but he reminds me how so many of us who are Christians *say* we believe but act as if it's all a big myth. A nice story, this Bible stuff, but come on … And that's why we are so powerless. Our lack of strength comes from our lack of certainty that we serve a God who can do anything. We become stronger when we fully understand how strong and powerful God is.

I'll admit it's hard to believe. All of it. Jesus raising Lazarus from the dead. Moses making the sun stand still. The Noah story. How would you get a couple of ants onto a boat? And fruit flies? And of course it was a wooden boat, so a couple of termites seem like a bad idea. How would you get them on there? On the other hand, if you believe in a Creator, then it's not so far-fetched. You and I couldn't pull it off. But if a Creator can make two ants, couldn't he also get them to walk onto a boat?

I know that may be difficult to understand. I can't create. You can't either. Try it! Not one molecule, not a single atom. And yet, when we're talking about God speaking our world into existence, it's not hard to realize that these stories in the Bible actually could happen. If God is the Creator, and he made this world, then obviously he can make anything happen upon this earth. *His* earth.

We have to understand: if in the beginning God created the heavens and the earth, then what can't he do? Psalm 115:3 says it so clearly: "Our God is in the heavens. He does all that he pleases." God does whatever he wants. The Bible says he's not like us. I could desire to do something, but that doesn't mean I can pull it off. But there is a being who does whatever he desires. In Daniel 4:34–35, King Nebuchadnezzar says about God, "His dominion is an everlasting dominion, and his kingdom endures from generation to generation; all the inhabitants of the earth are accounted as nothing, and he does according to his will among the host of heaven and among the inhabitants of the earth; and none can stay his hand or say to him, 'What have you done?'"

The Bible says that in heaven, there's a being who, if you could gather every single person on the earth together into one spot, that would be as nothing to him. Who can hold back his hand? Who could say to him, "Who do you think you are? You can't tell me what to do"? Because we don't talk enough about the power of God, we live in a generation of arrogant people who think they don't answer to anyone. But we have to consider the difference between a creator and his created being.

Let's say I could make a little human being right now out of thin air. I could hold him in my hand. I would be his creator, and he would be my creation. Now imagine I'm holding him in my palm, admiring my work, and he says to me, "You don't own me! I can do what I want. Who do you think you are?" There's a huge gap between the created thing and the creator. Like the Scripture says, how could the tiny man hold back his creator's hand? This is why you could gather together millions of these tiny people, and they'd appear as nothing before their creator. God is that Creator. God is that Maker. No one can say to him, "What have you done?"

And yet we do it all the time. We question him: "Why did you do that this way? Why didn't you do what I wanted?" The answer is because he wants to. He's God, he's in heaven, and he can do whatever he wants. He doesn't need your permission. He doesn't need anyone's permission. God is allowed to do things even if you don't understand them. We don't think about that enough. When God does something, that makes it right. That makes it just. God doesn't do things *because* they're just. They *are* just because it's *him* doing them. I can't say to God, "Here are the rules. Here's what's fair. You have to stay within these parameters." No, he sets the parameters.

I heard one of my favorite quotes, ever, probably fifteen to twenty years ago. I was driving in my car, listening to this old preacher, J. Vernon McGee, on the radio. He's long since passed away, but he was this old-timey pastor with kind of a high-pitched, "old man" voice that I just loved listening to. I'll never forget what he said:

"This is God's universe, and God does things his way. You may have a better way, but you don't have a universe."

That's so perfect. It just sums it all up, doesn't it? Maybe you think it's not fair that God created hell, a place of punishment. Maybe you think he shouldn't have made it eternal. Maybe you've thought, *You can't give me desires and then tell me not to do those things.* We all have different ideas of what God ought to do. You think you know what you'd do if you were God. J. Vernon says, "Great! When you get a universe, do it your way. But for now, this is God's universe. And no one holds back his hand."

We have to accept that God does what he wants. We need to have a sense of reverence for his power. In 1 Timothy 6:15 – 16, Paul reminds Timothy, "He who is the blessed and only Sovereign, the King of kings and Lord of lords, who alone has immortality, who dwells in unapproachable light, whom no one has ever seen or can see. To him be honor and eternal dominion. Amen."

Only one being is like that. None of us have control. Only one has absolute control: the King of kings and Lord of lords. It doesn't matter how successful or powerful you think you are. He's the king over you, the one lord, no matter who you are. He's the only sovereign.

He alone holds immortality. I can take a breath only because he lets me. He controls this thing called life. He determines whether you'll walk out of the room you're in right now. Only he can give life. He's the only one who takes it away. Everything's up to him. Do you understand that Satan is alive only because God allows him to be? One being possesses all power, all life. Every demon would die the moment he chooses to take their life away. He alone is immortal.

So what are you going to say to *that* God? Are you going to tell him he's not allowed to do something? We've become so arrogant because we've forgotten that only one being gives life, one is sovereign, one is in control. It's only by his grace that we breathe. The Bible says that he dwells in unapproachable light. He's clothed in light. If we were to try to look directly at him, we would die. No human being can look at him and live. Only one being dwells in unapproachable light like that, has all control, and is immortal. Only one true ruler is king over all of us. And yet, we can start to feel so self-important that we question him. We forget his power. No one has seen or can see him. To him be honor and eternal dominion.

At around Easter, I was studying Philippians 2, about Christ coming down and then returning to take his rightful place. It cross-referenced this passage in the Old Testament, Isaiah 45:22 – 23: "Turn to me and be saved, all the ends of the earth! For I am God, and there is no other. By myself I have sworn; from my mouth has gone out in righteousness a word that shall not return: 'To me every knee shall bow, every tongue shall swear allegiance.'"

God says here, "I'm the only God, so turn to me and you'll be saved." He also makes the statement, "By myself I have sworn." Some translations say, "I swear to myself." You shouldn't swear. I don't advocate swearing. Don't swear. But those naughty people who *do* swear, what do they say? They say, "I swear to God," right?

God himself says, "I swear to myself." That's pretty awesome. What would you swear by? We want to swear by the greatest power in existence. It's amazing—we have a God in heaven who says, "I swear to myself because there's nothing greater. I am the only God."

He continues, "From my mouth has gone out in righteousness a word that shall not return." In other words, he says, "When I say something will happen, it happens." When you and I say something's going to happen, it's maybe fifty-fifty. We don't ultimately have control. But God does. He says, "When I say something, it happens. I swear by myself. It's coming from my mouth, so you know it will happen."

He continues, "To me, every knee shall bow, every tongue shall swear allegiance." What he's saying here is, "I swear to you by my own name, and when I say something, it happens. One day, every single created thing is going to bow to me. Everyone will acknowledge that I am God."

I don't know what that does for you. There was a time in my Christian walk when I was almost afraid of that power. But now, it's my greatest security. If that God is for me, who can be against me? By not talking about the power of God, we lose our security. I'm going to look pretty stupid while I live on this earth. Because of my morality, because of what I believe, and because I trust in the Bible, I'll look dumb to a lot of people. I'll talk about this Jesus who died for their sins, and many people will reject it. But I know that the day will arrive when this God is going to come. I'm on his side, so I'm going to bow now. Our God is that powerful. He put his Spirit in us. As his children, we should have courage.

Joshua 1:6−9 says, "Be strong and courageous, for you shall cause this people to inherit the land that I swore to their fathers to give them. Only be strong and very courageous, being careful to do according to all the law that Moses my servant commanded you. Do not turn from it to the right hand or to the left, that you may have good success wherever you go. This Book of the Law shall not depart from your mouth, but you shall meditate on it day and night, so that you may be careful to do according to all that is written in it. For then you will make your way prosperous, and then you will have good success. Have I not commanded you? Be strong and courageous. Do not be frightened, and do not be dismayed, for the Lord your God is with you wherever you go."

Over and over again, God tells Joshua, "Be strong and courageous. Be strong and courageous. Be strong and courageous. Be strong and very courageous. Don't be afraid." Strength and courage should typify us, characterize us, define us. Because of the Spirit that's inside of us, we should not be afraid.

Some days I feel discouraged, even defeated. My church friends sometimes slip their arm around me, cry with me, and say things like,

"I'm so sorry. I know it's tough."

"Why don't you take a vacation?"

"Maybe you need more family time."

"You should get more sleep."

I'm longing for the day when someone instead says to me, "Francis, you know what? You're a powerful person. The Holy Spirit of God is inside you. I know things are difficult. But be strong and courageous."

I don't know many believers who gather together and encourage each other to be strong. Peter and John astonished people with their boldness, and yet when they got out of jail, they prayed for more boldness! In Ephesians 6:19−20, Paul, the boldest guy on earth, says, "Pray for me, that I can preach the word boldly." The body of Christ needs once again to lay hands on each other, praying for boldness and strength. We should remind each other that we serve an almighty God. He's coming back, and every knee will bow. He swore to himself that it's going to happen. We may look stupid now, but we need to stay on his side and do everything his Word says. Let's live it. Let's walk it. Let's urge each other on toward boldness, power, strength. The church of Jesus Christ should once again be known as strong, bold, and courageous.

# CHAPTER 2

# G O D
# IS HERE

*Dino Rizzo*

Life is full of moments we can't predict. We make plans and have a pretty good idea of how we'd like to see things turn out. And then our plans go right out the window. Things happen that we never could have imagined. Life goes that way, but no matter what happens, we can count on one thing: God is right there with us.

When I was twenty-three, I was invited to conduct a revival. This was a great opportunity for a young preacher. A real revival. I had been doing youth camps and helping out with other youth meetings, but never a real, "big church" revival. And then out of the blue I got a call from a church in Houma, Louisiana—down in the bayou country. I'm talking deep south in the marshes and swamps of Louisiana. I was so excited, because they said, "We want you to come in on a Sunday, and speak in the morning, and then again on Sunday night, and if the meetings go well, we're going to extend them through the week."

This was big time for me. I'd never had anything like that happen before. So I started imagining what this revival was going to be like. Big crowds of people who would be inspired by my preaching and the music. They would tell all their friends about it and more would come back on Sunday night and they would decide to extend the meeting into the week. I'd heard stories about revivals where people were standing outside the church, lining up to get inside. I was excited about preaching at my first revival!

When I finally got to the address of the church that Sunday morning, all I saw was a small storefront. Not exactly what I had in mind, but it didn't matter. I was there to preach about Jesus and it didn't make any difference to me if it was in a cathedral or a tar-paper shack. The pastor met me as I got out of the car and led me inside the storefront church, where there were some small plastic chairs arranged in a circle.

"Let's have church," he announced to the ten or so people who had shown up.

And we did. No praise band or instruments or video screens with the words printed out against a pretty background. The pastor just started singing and everyone joined in. Except I didn't know the words and couldn't really fake it because we were sitting in a circle and everyone was looking at me. I just sort of hummed along until something interrupted the service. This dear, precious lady, who was obviously going through a difficult time, started making some strange sounds. She just had that look on her face that something was going on inside of her that was really bad. I didn't know what was going on, and my heart went out to her, but she just kept making these strange sounds and pretty soon she was on the floor, writhing and squirming and getting louder in her anguish.

The pastor looked at me and said, "You're the evangelist. Fix it."

Everyone sitting in that small circle was now looking at me. My mind started racing and I knew I had only a few seconds to figure out what to do. I had not anticipated anything like this would happen; I was supposed to preach a gospel message and see people saved. I saw the pain on her face and realized there was something dark going on in her life. This was what people call a spiritual battle, but I didn't know what I was supposed to do. I'm sure I had read books on spiritual warfare and probably had preached about it to young people. But this was for real. When I woke up that morning, I had no idea I would be standing beside a woman who was shrieking and writhing on the floor at my revival meeting.

"Are you going to handle this?" The pastor seemed impatient.

I knew I had to do something. I *wanted* to do something, I really did. I just didn't know what to do. As I knelt down beside her, I prayed, "Jesus, help me. Help us."

And that's when I realized I didn't have to fix this all by myself. Even as I wondered what to do next, I sensed the Lord whispering into my heart, "I have already taken care of this at the cross. Whatever her need is, whatever her situation is, whatever the pain is, whatever the darkness is, whatever spiritual battle she's going through, I've already handled it. Just lift up my name and she'll be fine." I leaned over that hurting child of God and prayed in the name of Jesus for whatever was causing her such anguish, and guess what? Jesus was true to his word. The woman grew calm, and that look of fear and pain left her face. I truly believe God began healing her in that very moment. He reassured her that he loved her, something she once might have believed could never be possible. In that moment, God began to pour out his power on her life. Right there in Houma, Louisiana, where I had planned to start a big revival, we had a God moment. She even left to bring some friends back to the storefront church, and we had a great time praising God for what he did in her life that morning. It could have been the only reason I was invited to that little church to hold a revival.

That experience of praying for one woman who was in the middle of a battle for her soul was not what I expected, it was not what I planned for, but it was better than anything I might have planned because of what it did in my life and the faith that it built inside of me. It gave me the confidence to trust Jesus more than I trust myself and to know that he is always right there with me, no matter what kind of situation I get myself into.

Don't get me wrong: I'm all for planning and doing our best to serve God with our talents. I might have gotten a little carried away with thinking how that revival would turn out, but I was serious about serving God. I had my sermons prepared and was ready to go the distance. I wanted to preach so effectively that hundreds — maybe thousands — would give their hearts to Jesus. But he had something else in mind. That woman's soul was more important to God at that moment than my plans to do big things for him.

As our churches get bigger and better and more sophisticated, it's tempting to think it all depends on us. That for God to "succeed," he needs us to prepare the best sermons and build the biggest churches. We begin to act like Martha when Jesus wants us to be more like Mary. Remember the story? Martha invited Jesus to her house and when he arrived, she spent all her time preparing the meal and everything so that it would go exactly as she had planned. Her sister, Mary, on the other hand, just sat and listened to what Jesus had to say. Jesus told Martha, "Mary has chosen what is better."

We want to do a lot of good things in our churches, but Jesus wants to do better things. We have armies of people—paid staff and volunteers—to make sure the sound system is set at the right level, the PowerPoint slides are in the right order, the musicians are ready, the greeters are at their places, and the lighting is just right. Everything is coordinated, orchestrated, choreographed, and planned for a great outcome, and that's good. God has given us all these wonderful tools and talented people for a purpose, and I know he uses them for his glory. But what if sometimes his agenda is different from the one we have planned? What if he wants to do something really wild, unlike anything he's ever done before? He's always present when we gather to worship, but things will just keep going according to *our* plans if we don't really believe he's there and leave some room for him to interrupt us.

There's a brief story in Mark's gospel that shows us how anything can happen when Jesus is present. He was in the vicinity of the city of Tyre when some people approached him with a man who was deaf and couldn't speak well. What happens next tells us a lot about Jesus: "After he took him aside, away from the crowd, Jesus put his fingers into the man's ears. Then he spit and touched the man's tongue. He looked up to heaven and with a deep sigh said to him, '*Ephphatha!*' (which means, 'Be opened!'). At this, the man's ears were opened, his tongue was loosed and he began to speak plainly and clearly. Jesus commanded them not to tell anyone. [This is amazing.] But the more he did so, the more they kept talking about it. People were overwhelmed with amazement" (Mark 7:33–37).

When Jesus is present, faith happens. Somehow, the people who brought the deaf man to Jesus knew something unexpected could happen. They knew of his power, most likely based on reports they had heard of this man who could heal people. They came to Jesus with great expectations and believed that it was not going to be business as usual. When they learned that Jesus was going to be in their area, they got all fired up—maybe took the day off just to take their friend to him because they *knew* something great would happen. Because of the resurrection, Jesus is always present, which means we too can expect the unexpected to happen in our lives. We don't have to check out his travel schedule to see where he's going to be. He's here! Imagine how things might change in our churches if we truly believed that *anything* could happen because Jesus is with us. I love it when people come to church believing, "I wonder what's going to happen today." But too many times, we just do church like we always do church and then wonder why nothing special happens.

What I also love about this story is that when Jesus is present, love happens. Jesus always responds in a way that is perfect for the situation. He does that because of his compassion. This deaf man's friends asked Jesus to lay hands on him right there in the middle of the road. But the Bible says Jesus pulled the man aside, and I believe that was because he wanted to make this poor individual feel at ease, to avoid the embarrassment of having everyone watch what was going on. Have you ever gone to the doctor and when you check in the nurse asks you—usually in a loud voice—what you need to see the doctor about? And you're standing there with a room full of people waiting and you just know they're going to hear every word you say. Here Jesus anticipated this man's embarrassment and out of love, pulled him away from the crowd.

Maybe I'm making too big a deal of this because of what I experienced as a child. I grew up with a speech challenge—didn't talk until I was three years old. People couldn't really understand me when I tried to talk, so I was sent to a special kindergarten where they tested me and then sent me to speech therapy every day. Back in those days they weren't as sensitive about these things like they are now, so it was just, "Send the Rizzo kid to resource class," and you had to get up in front of everyone and leave the classroom and everyone knew why.

Jesus protected this deaf man, who couldn't talk very well, the same way my mom protected me when one of my teachers made us do oral reports. Can you imagine a kid who stutters and can't speak clearly having to stand up in front of everyone and give an oral report? My mom heard about it and drove to the school and just got into that teacher's face and told her, "He's not going to do any oral report," and that was it. That's what Jesus did for this man—he protected his dignity. When Jesus is present, we never have to worry about being embarrassed, because he loves us so much. He knows exactly what we need, and however he chooses to meet that need, it will be perfect.

When I preach about this story, I take a little liberty and tell people that the third thing we can expect when Jesus is present is this: spit happens. It always gets a big laugh, but it's really just a way to help them remember that Jesus "spoke" to this man with sign language. He knew the guy was deaf, so talking to him would have been useless. So he touched his ears, letting him know he was going to make him hear again. Then he touched his tongue and looked up toward heaven. I believe he was reassuring the guy in a language he could understand: "I'm going to call on my Father in heaven to open your ears and help you speak clearly."

So what about the spit? Come on—if you grew up when I did, you would know that spit is a cure-all. Maybe moms don't do this now, but if my face was dirty, my momma would lick her fingers and give me a spit bath on the way to church. If I fell down and skinned my knee, my daddy would spit on his hand and rub it into my wound as if it had some magical healing power. And it worked!

So maybe Jesus used his spit because he knew this guy had a momma and a daddy like mine. That when he spit on his hand it told this guy that just like your momma used to smooth down your cowlick before you went to school, I'm going to fix you the same way. Maybe not. But when Jesus is here, anything can happen, right?

The last thing that I take away from this story about the deaf man is that when Jesus is present, hope happens. I can just see this man, sheltered from the crowd as Jesus reaches toward him. He hears Jesus sigh as he looks heavenward, and at that moment, this man who could not hear and could not speak clearly was filled with hope. "Maybe this is really going to work. Maybe before the day is over I'm going to be able to hear people when they speak." And I believe that when Jesus said, "Be opened," the man heard the word *opened* and it changed his life. The very first word he heard was Jesus saying "opened." When you lose hope, you lose everything, but when Jesus is present, you always have hope.

What an amazing miracle. That man got up that day having no idea where his friends were taking him. And he had an encounter with Jesus Christ, the Son of God, and something so out of the ordinary happened. Power changed the man's problem, but it was love that transformed his life. Jesus could have snapped his fingers and the man would have been healed instantly, but he chose to treat the man with dignity and to minister to him because he loved him. And even though Jesus asked him and his friends to keep quiet about what happened, they couldn't. They were "overwhelmed with amazement" and told everyone they ran into about this amazing experience that occurred all because Jesus was present.

That's what happens when we believe God is present and we let him do whatever he wants.

Have you ever planned a trip or a meeting and something happened that wasn't part of your plan? Like maybe you are trying to get to an important conference in another city and you miss your connection and have to cool your heels for several hours. Or maybe you have your schedule for the day all set and then you get a call from someone who insists he needs to meet with you. Right now. I know those things can be annoying, but what if we chose instead to look for Jesus in those interruptions? What if we viewed them as opportunities to see what Jesus is doing and wants to do *through* us? Jesus might have felt pressure to spend time with Martha because she had gone to all the trouble of preparing for his visit, but instead he sat and talked with Mary. Martha had her plans; Mary just wanted Jesus. Waiting for a plane in a crowded airport can be a pain in the neck. Or it could be an opportunity for an engaging conversation with that one person who needs to be with Jesus, and you're the only one in the entire airport who can make the introduction.

When that lady started making strange noises and crawling around on the floor at my first revival meeting, I was afraid. Afraid that it would disrupt our planned revival. Afraid because I didn't know what to do. Afraid because it was out of my control. Afraid because I was all alone.

But in my fear, I called out to God and realized I *wasn't* alone. He was right there beside me. He always is, but just be ready. Because when God is present, anything can happen. And God is always present.

CHAPTER 3

# G O D
## IS INCOMPARABLE

### *Mark Batterson*

*I pray also that the eyes of your heart may be enlightened in order
that you may know the hope to which he has called you, the riches
of his glorious inheritance in the saints, and his incomparably
great power for us who believe.*

— Ephesians 1:18–19

Most people remember speeches because of what was said or who
said it. But I remember this particular lecture because of where it
was delivered. As a freshman at the University of Chicago, I took a
class where I spent most of the semester nodding my head, not in
agreement with what the professor said but in a colossal struggle to
stay awake. But what caught my attention one particular afternoon
was the revelation from our professor that just a few feet from our
lecture hall was the spot where Enrico Fermi, on December 2, 1942,
unleashed the power of the atom by splitting it.

We were practically standing on scientific hallowed ground!
The technical term for what Fermi accomplished is *nuclear fission* and
the full impact of that discovery was felt on August 6, 1945, when

the *Enola Gay* dropped the first atomic bomb over Hiroshima, Japan. It took forty-three seconds for that bomb to fall thirty-one thousand feet. A barometric switch triggered the first subatomic reaction, and in a matter of a few millionths of a second, the heat at the core of that bomb reached a temperature of several million degrees Celsius. When the bomb exploded at 8:16:02 local time, four square miles of that city were devastated. Sixty-six thousand people lost their lives without even knowing what was coming as silent shock waves reverberated at the speed of sound. Buildings were leveled six miles away, glass was broken twelve miles away, and the energy produced by that bomb, the glare from that blast, was so powerful that it would have been visible from Jupiter, roughly 390 million miles away. Those statistics are staggering, but here is what is almost inconceivable: the energy produced by that bomb was the byproduct of a subatomic reaction that used only one percent of two pounds of uranium; one third of an ounce of uranium was sucked out of existence, and it translated into an explosion two thousand times more powerful than the most powerful bomb in the history of warfare.

Fermi's successful experiment owes a lot to Albert Einstein. It was more than a century ago that Einstein published what may be the most recognizable equation in the realm of science, $E = mc^2$ (energy equals mass multiplied by the speed of light squared). Now, the speed of light squared is such a large number that really, in a simple translation, it simply means this: there is an awful lot of energy in a very small amount of matter. The amount of potential energy in every invisible atom is almost inconceivable.

If the amount of energy in every subatomic particle is virtually inconceivable, then how can we even begin to comprehend the potential energy of an omnipotent Creator who created all matter? We can't. And that is the point of Paul's prayer in Ephesians. He combines two Greek superlatives and says God's power is not just great, God's power is not just incomparable, but God's power is incomparably great. There is no comparison.

## GOD IS INCOMPARABLE

We tend to think about God in human terms. We do that, of course, because we are human. In the beginning, God created us in *his* image, but we've been creating God in *our* image ever since. That's not necessarily bad, because it helps us get our arms around something so big that otherwise we couldn't grasp it. The term for doing this is *anthropomorphism*, the attribution of human characteristics to God. For example, we tend to think of God in four-dimensional terms because that's all we have ever known. We cannot conceive of anything beyond our four dimensions of space and time, so what we do is project our four dimensions of space-time limitations on God, and what we end up with is a God who is a little bigger, a little better, a little stronger, and a little wiser than we are. We end up with a God who is a supersized version of ourselves. We think that God's power is slightly more powerful than the most powerful thing we can imagine. We think of God's grace as slightly more gracious than the most gracious thing we can imagine. We think of God's wisdom as slightly wiser than the wisest person we've ever known.

The problem with thinking of God this way is that it makes God too small. And when we have a small god, we don't expect him to do big things. Paul's image of God is correct: "God is incomparably great." There is simply no comparison when it comes to describing God.

## PUTTING GOD IN A WET SUIT

I was in Southern California recently speaking at a conference near Seal Beach, which brought back a funny memory from the first time I had been there about ten years earlier. I had been there with my two brothers-in-law, Rob and Joel, and we decided to go boogie boarding. The water in the Pacific Ocean was really cold that day, so this pastor friend we were hanging out with got us some wet suits … from three junior high kids. Those suits were so small it took ten minutes for Joel and me to get ours on. But Rob was a pretty big guy, so Joel and I had to pull and yank on his sleeves and pant legs because he was so big and the suit was so small. It probably didn't help that we were laughing so hard we could barely stand up. We finally got him tucked into his neoprene straight jacket, but he couldn't zip it up, so as soon as he hit the water, the suit filled up and he sank to the bottom like a beluga whale. I'm laughing again as I imagine big old Rob in that tiny little suit, but that's exactly what we do to God. We put a little junior higher's wet suit on him. We try to bring God down to our level, and if it weren't so sad and detrimental to our spiritual health, it might be funny.

Every problem we experience is a byproduct of our small view of God. Conversely, once you understand God's incomparable nature, your problems lose their dominance over you. They may not disappear — life is full of problems we can't avoid — but they won't control you. A proper view of God enables you to transcend all the barriers that get in your way. I've known wealthy people who lose some value in their stocks or experience a financial setback and it just about kills them. They can't stop thinking about how bad the market is and what it's doing to their investments. I've also known people whom you and I would consider dirt poor but who seemed so grateful for what little they had that their contentment was infectious. One saw God as too small to provide for them; the other knew God owned the cattle on a thousand hills and would make sure they always had enough.

I've also known people who received the diagnosis of an incurable disease. Some go into an absolute panic and become depressed and even angry at God for allowing it to happen. Then there are those who believe that the Great Physician can heal them if he chooses to do so, and if he doesn't, they take comfort in knowing they have an eternal reward in heaven, where they will never be sick again. Who serves the bigger God? The late A. W. Tozer, a popular preacher and bestselling author, once wrote, "A low view of God is the cause of a hundred lesser evils. A high view of God is the solution to 10,000 temporal problems." In other words, if you want to live a victorious life, let God out of your tiny wet suit.

The problem with having a small view of God is that we don't expect much from him. We pray timidly, asking him to bless us or provide for us, never really daring to put our faith on the line in a dramatic fashion. We accept a life that is just a little better than it could be rather than expecting a life the Bible describes as abundant. Abundant means more than enough. An incomparably great God wants to give you more than enough, whether it's in your marriage, your job, your relationship with your family, or your overall sense of fulfillment. This is God you're praying to. Incomparable. There's nothing like him. We can't even begin to comprehend his power. He can do anything and desires to lavish you with his blessings. But if we squeeze him into our tiny wet suits, we settle for "just a little better."

When you try to imagine what God looks like, what comes to mind? For me, it's usually a painting. I love all the different paintings of Jesus that depict him in different settings. The ones that I usually "see" when I try to think of what God looks like include Jesus with the lost lamb draped around his neck and Jesus standing at the door and knocking. The artists accurately captured God's relentless pursuit of his fallen children — you and me. I think every grandparent has one of those pictures hanging in their living rooms. Another favorite for many is Jesus on the cross. We are drawn to that because it reminds us of the enormous sacrifice he undertook on our behalf. But while I love these images of Jesus, I think we need another one. Maybe it already exists, but I haven't seen it. The painting we need is one that shows Jesus seated on a throne in heaven, because that image demonstrates his victory over death. It graphically reminds us of his power and authority — a triumphant Jesus, the Son of the incomparable God. When we begin to understand that there is absolutely no power on earth that comes close to his power — and that it is available to us — we will begin to live as if we are "more than conquerors."

## IT'S NOT ABOUT YOU

Recently I renewed my health club membership. At this particular gym, they offer you a free session with a trainer when you renew. Since I really wanted to get in shape, I took advantage of their offer. What was I thinking? This guy put me through a twenty minute routine that just about killed me. I had worked out with weights in the past, but he had me doing resistance exercises, crunches, lunges, pull-ups — things I'd never done before. I couldn't even do all the reps he asked me to do, and I almost threw up before I finished. Four days later I was still sore. I asked the guy why these exercises hurt so much, and he told me that when most people exercise, they work on their extremities, but if you really want to get into proper shape, you need to work on your core. The exercises he had me doing focused on those core muscles. He said that once those were strengthened, I could move on to the extremities. Those guys with the huge biceps who strut around the gym may look great, he told me, but they're just muscle-bound. They're really not that strong because their core muscles are weak.

A lot of us who love Jesus are like that. We work on our spiritual gifts. We make sure we are consistent with our daily devotions. We try to witness and make decisions based on solid biblical principles. Most of the time, we look pretty good. But the first wind that comes along knocks us over because our "core spiritual muscles" are weak. Our image of God is so small that despite all our good spiritual activity, it doesn't sustain us when the going gets tough.

When we make God just a little bigger than ourselves, he's easier to ignore, and soon we fall into that dangerous zone of thinking it's all about us. We become self-reliant because we don't really believe God is big enough for what's the matter. Of course, none of us will admit this, but just look at the way you live. Can you say burnout? How many people do you know who have poured themselves into God's work only to run out of steam, get discouraged, and quit? I have a prayer that I pray frequently: "Lord, I can't do this alone." It may sound like a goofy prayer because, of course, God knows that, but it's my way of saying that I'm not smart enough, I'm not strong enough, I'm not big enough to do his work. I need his help. I need his power. Without it, I am nothing. Compared with his strength, I'm a weakling.

When we fully understand God's incomparable greatness, we realize that without him we can do nothing but that with him we can do anything. It changes us from being spiritual wimps to spiritual giants. It's what gave a little sheepherder the courage to take on Goliath, and it will empower you to take on any challenge that you face.

I'm always fascinated to hear how people come to Christ, and I was struck recently by the story of Yann Martel, the author of *Life of Pi*. He grew up an atheist, but during the process of writing that best-selling, prizewinning book, he came to faith in God. Describing his transition into belief, he said, "I was sick to death of reasonableness."

Reason tells us that we don't have enough money to afford a missions trip. That your antagonistic neighbor will never be interested in learning about Jesus. That your marriage will always be a struggle. That life as you are currently experiencing it is as good as it gets. We sprinkle a little bit of prayer and the Bible and church on our lives and hope. Hope is good, but expectation is better.

When you believe in God's incomparable power, your hopes change to great expectations.

# CHAPTER 4

# G O D

# IS RECONCILER

## *Clark Mitchell*

I remember that Tuesday morning in September 2008 like it was yesterday. I was in my office at the church when I got the call from my dad's doctor. He said my dad had taken a turn for the worse and they were moving him to the intensive care unit. On my way out the door, I looked at some of the pastors on my staff with tears in my eyes. I was headed for a moment that no one can ever prepare to experience.

After spending some time with my dad, I saw his doctor standing at the nurse's station. In my typical self-reliant, overconfident (and sometimes arrogant) way, I walked up to the doctor to discuss the situation. A few minutes into our conversation, I cut him off: "I'm a straight shooter; so let's get right to the point. Is my dad going to live?" I had always viewed myself as pretty tough, but it was at that exact moment that God began to radically change my life.

The doctor must have believed me because he didn't pull any punches: "Your father has a week to live, at best." I held my composure for a few minutes as he went on about his condition. When I simply couldn't take it any longer, I abruptly told him I had to get back to my office and quickly walked out of the ICU. On my way to the elevator, I acknowledged those I passed with a semblance of normalcy, yet what was going on inside of me was anything but normal. I held it together until I reached my car, where I totally lost it. How could this be happening? My dad would be gone by the end of the week.

In the coming days, I felt the love of my church staff and friends in a supernatural way; I saw the church functioning as it was intended; I felt the love of God in a deeper way than ever before; and I had an encounter with God that would change the rest of my life.

# MAKING UP THE DIFFERENCE

I grew up in a picture-perfect family. Every week after church, my family would walk down the tree-lined streets of our neighborhood to my grandparents' house for Sunday lunch. Right before I started the sixth grade, we moved to a new town and, like clockwork, my parents accepted a friend's invitation to go to church. Not long after we began attending, I made the decision to "walk the aisle" and trust Christ with my life. It was in that church that my faith would be shaped in a tremendous way; I would learn to pray, learn to worship, learn to give, learn about community, learn the Word, but most important, I would learn that God loves me.

I was also challenged with Scripture Memory. As students, we were encouraged to memorize Scripture for our own well-being. However, what really drove us was the Super Bowl of Scripture Memory — the ultimate Christian throwdown that took place once a year. With guys on one side of the room and girls on the other, the competition would begin. Here's the first Bible passage I memorized: "Therefore, if anyone is in Christ, he is a new creation; the old has gone, the new has come! All this is from God, who reconciled us to himself through Christ.... We implore you on Christ's behalf: Be reconciled to God. God made him who had no sin to be sin for us, so that in him we might become the righteousness of God" (2 Cor. 5:17–21).

Who doesn't love the "new creation" story? It's the passage I've retreated to thousands of times throughout my life when I've needed to pump myself up. Whenever the enemy has been messing with me or I'm feeling kind of down about myself or maybe I've even (dare I say it?) sinned, what do I do? I pull out the new-creation mantra.

I've said it over and over, but for some reason, there are times when it just doesn't seem to do the trick.

Growing up in church, the one thing I never got tired of was the Gossip Circle, a fun-filled game where everyone sits in a circle with all their friends and one person is chosen to start a story. The person who begins the story whispers it to the person next to them, and the process continues until the story makes it all the way around the circle. By the time the story gets to the end of the circle, there might be a little bit of the truth left, but for the most part, the original story has changed.

That's exactly what happened to me! This God-loving, church-going, Scripture-memorizing, TBN-watching, Christian-music-listening, veteran "Christian" had missed the meaning behind Paul's important teaching about our relationship with God. How was it that while I knew a little bit of the truth, I had missed so much of its fruit? Even though I had known God's forgiveness, I had never experienced the freedom and joy that come from being reconciled. As I wrestled with the grief of losing my father, for the first time I met God the reconciler.

At the end of each day, bank employees count the cash in their registers and check it against the printed records of their transactions, and if there is a difference between the two amounts, they have to make up that difference, or reconcile it. That's exactly what God does when we accept his free gift of salvation—he makes up the difference between our sinfulness and his holiness. The meaning I had missed in the new-creation story is that God adjusted my differences with him so that I could be received by him with favor. It's not just that God loves me, which I learned as a youngster, but that he *approves* of me. He affirms me. I really am a new person, not just a cleaned up version of the old one. Once you believe this, it changes your entire relationship with God.

## DON'T LOOK BACK

Many of us would say we approach God through our praying, serving, giving, and worship. All of those are definitely things we do *as* we approach him, but they doesn't answer the question of *how* we should approach him. The book of Hebrews gives us a pretty straightforward clue: "Therefore, brothers, since we have confidence to enter the Most Holy Place by the blood of Jesus, by a new and living way opened for us through the curtain, that is, his body, and since we have a great priest over the house of God, let us draw near to God with a sincere heart" (Heb. 10:19–22). I love that thought! Approaching the throne of God with a little bit of attitude, an attitude you can receive only from having your heavenly Father's affirmation, by experiencing the Father's favor.

So what's holding us back? I'll tell you. It's us! *We* are holding *ourselves* back! In fact, Scripture says they "*exchanged* the truth of God for a lie." Today many of us approach God believing lies about ourselves. We base our identity on what others say about us rather than what God says about us and miss out on the freedom that comes with reconciliation. It's like the time I was running in freshman gym class. At 6' 3" and 130 pounds, I looked like a praying mantis in my 1980s jogging shorts, but since I was leading the pack on our daily run outside, I was pretty proud of myself. I decided to look back and do the "cool wave" at a couple of cute girls who I knew were bringing up the rear when it hit me. Literally. I ran into a stop sign. I went from showing off for the girls to lying flat on the ground with blood streaming down my face.

Looking back can be dangerous.

For many of us, the same thing has happened in our relationship with God. We start running after God and somewhere along the line, we hit a stop sign. The reason? We're looking over our shoulders to see what the gossip circle is saying about us. And at some point, we begin to believe the lie. We start believing what our parents have said about us, what our friends have said about us, what our ex-boyfriend or ex-girlfriend has said about us, what our husband or wife has said about us, and all of a sudden, we hit a stop sign. We start basing our relationship with God on gossip and not the gospel.

We look back at who we used to be, when God has already made up the difference for us. We start believing that even though we've been forgiven, we're still not good enough. So we try harder and then hit that sign again. I had been the kind of Christian who thought my relationship with God depended on being good enough, and in my grief, God showed me that I had really been living spiritually as a slave when all along I was his son.

Through years of studying the Word, watching others, and my own experiences, I've realized we can approach God in one of two ways: we can approach him either as a slave or as his sons and daughters.

Slaves base their relationships with their masters on their performance. It's the only way they can receive affirmation or favor. As followers of Christ, many of us approach our relationships with God as slaves. For whatever reason, we feel that if we can just "perform well enough," somehow this gap might be closed in and God will love us more. We live our daily lives thinking, *If I can just perform well enough, then God will be pleased and he'll love me.* We have failed to understand reconciliation and are trying to make up the difference all by ourselves. If we get on a roll of good performance, we're on a spiritual high, thinking God must really be pleased with us. So something like a quiet time of devotion with God becomes a duty to check off rather than a privilege to be enjoyed. But inevitably, our performance suffers. We skip devotions or fail to witness to someone, and we sink into a spiritual depression, thinking God is displeased and maybe even angry and so we've got to just work harder to get back in his favor.

This is why so many Christians describe their spiritual lives as a roller coaster. Or in my case, a ski slope.

## YOU'LL NEVER MEASURE UP

About once every three years, I take my family snow skiing. I'm not really sure why, because I hate skiing. Snow skiing is one of the only times when I cuss. I don't think preachers should cuss, either, but it happens on every ski trip.

Here's why I hate skiing. In my mind, I'm the best at whatever I'm considering doing. If I'm watching *Dancing with the Stars*, I'm the graceful guy who wins. If I'm watching *American Idol*, there's no doubt in my mind that I can hit that high note perfectly. I'm just one of those guys who believes he can do anything, so when they have to stop the entire lift because I fell trying to escape the contraption, I get angry enough to make a preacher swear. My belief that I'm a great skier and my performance don't add up.

It took me way too long to learn that our beliefs and our performance will never measure up, and as far as God's concerned, that's okay. He still loves us when we fall down. He still affirms us and is pleased with us when we mess up. I now know that I don't have to be a perfect preacher who never cusses in order to receive God's favor. He's made up the difference between my potty mouth and his goodness. He'll do that for you as well.

The sinister thing about trying to earn God's favor is that it drives us to seek affirmation from others to convince us that we're worthy. We base our whole identity, our self-worth, on what others tell us, and that leads to an endless quest for whatever we think makes us look good. It's the reason why many of us want to drive nice cars. It's the reason we want to make great grades in school, to perform well on the team, to date the hottest girl or guy. We want to have people look at us and say, "Man, they've got it going on!" We're simply seeking affirmation, something we were created to need. The problem lies in the fact that we end up basing all of our relationships on our performance, including our relationship with God. We approach God as slaves thinking that good performance results in his favor and affirmation.

The beautiful message of the familiar parable of the prodigal son is that the wayward son never stopped being the son. When he finally returned, he was so ashamed of himself that he offered to become his father's slave. He thought he might be able to earn his way back into his father's favor. Even after his father greeted him with a hug and a kiss, the wayward son couldn't believe he was good enough. He even said, "I am no longer worthy to be called your son." So the father went the extra mile and ordered his servants to bring the best robe and a ring for his finger, signifying his status as a member of the family.

When we "come to our senses," as Scripture says, it's called repentance. Repentance is when we turn our faces to the Father and acknowledge our desire to relate with him. But the problem for many of us is we begin to approach him as slaves. We think, *I'm forgiven, but now I need to get my act together. If I perform well enough, I might get the favor of the Father.* But here's where it gets good. As soon as we turn our faces to him in repentance, the Father begins to take steps toward us as his sons and daughters! I am convinced that millions and millions of followers of Christ stop at repentance; they know they've been forgiven, but they never *experience* his favor. As a slave, you live in a place of repentance; as a son or daughter, you live in a place of restoration. As a slave, you live in a place of performance; as a son or daughter, you live in a place of peace. As a slave, you live in a place of hope; as a son or daughter, you live in a place of healing and wholeness.

Most of us approach God as a slave, not as a son or daughter. We allow our hurts to cause us to misconstrue the truth. My guess is many of us have fallen into the trap of the gossip circle and missed the original story. I know I did.

For many years, I allowed the enemy to mess with my mind, and I allowed the hurt from rejection to drive me to perform. For most of my life, I've been able to quote 2 Corinthians 5:17–21, but I wasn't experiencing the fullness of the truth in those verses. I was approaching God as a slave.

Maybe this is where you are. Maybe you never recovered from your parents' divorce, thinking you didn't do enough to save their marriage. Maybe you never recovered after your boyfriend dumped you in high school and the words written in his breakup letter ring true in your mind today. Maybe you started trying to perform at a higher level when your career didn't take off as fast as your friend's. Maybe you're a pastor and you come into the office on Monday defeated because you don't think your attendance is high enough. There could be a book full of maybes, but the truth remains: God is your reconciler!

You're not a slave but God's beloved child.

On that Tuesday afternoon in September, I put on my tough man act for the doctor as long as I could. But once I got in my car, I wept like a baby. I was so used to fixing any situation, but in this situation there was nothing I could fix. There was nothing I could do, and I believe that was when I began to see myself before God in a brand new light. I didn't have to *do* anything. My dad was a tremendous man of integrity and character, but he lived as a slave. Growing up, he had very low self-esteem and didn't feel the affirmation of his parents. He based his whole identity on his sense of failure and what he never became. He based his whole identity on rejection.

I will never forget the last conversation we had as I held his hand and he looked at me through his oxygen mask. Looking me in the eyes, he asked, "Clark, are you okay?" With tears in my eyes, I said, "Yeah, Dad, I am." A few moments passed, he squeezed my hand one last time and said, "Son, do you know how proud I am of you?" It was in that moment of grief that God began to heal my heart and free me from being a slave.

You see, my dad wasn't proud of me because of what I had done; he was proud of me because of who I was—his son. There is no doubt in my mind that if I were still at my first job putting pepperonis on pizzas at Little Caesars, his words would have been the same. There is no doubt that my dad was proud of my family, my kids, and the ministry God has allowed me to be involved in. But the love, favor, and affirmation my dad expressed to me wasn't based on any of those things or on how I had performed; it was based on who I was—his son.

Over the coming months, God used my grief to bring healing in my life, and I began to know God as my reconciler.

Maybe you've never heard this before, but God is proud of you. He knows you have some areas in your life that are a mess, but you're his child, and you can approach his throne with confidence because Christ made up the difference.

My one prayer for you today is that you would know in your heart that God is your reconciler. I pray that you will see the Father taking steps toward you. I pray that you'll be able to stop looking behind you and look forward to what God has for you. I pray that you'll begin with repentance and move on to restoration. I pray that you will not only know the Father's forgiveness but that you will also know his fullness and favor. I pray that you will put your hope in our big, big Savior and allow him to bring healing into your life. I pray that you release the words of rejection from the gossip circle and embrace the wholeness found in God. I pray that you will no longer spend your days performing, but rather spend them all in peace, knowing God is your reconciler!

# CHAPTER 5

# G O D

## IS CERTAIN

*Andy Stanley*

One of the most dramatic moments in the Bible, perhaps in all of human history, took place in an environment that we have come to refer to as "the upper room." It occurred toward the end of Jesus' ministry. Jesus and his disciples were going to Jerusalem to celebrate Passover, a Jewish festival that included a specific remembrance meal, a meal that commemorated what happened hundreds of years earlier when the Israelites ate their last meal as slaves in Egypt.

The Hebrew people had been in Egypt for four hundred years. They began as a family and grew into a nation. For their entire history, all they had known was slavery. They had prayed unceasingly to their God, but their prayers had gone unanswered for four hundred years. Finally, God sent a deliverer—Moses. He told them that they would be leaving the next day and that an angel of death was going to pass over Egypt that night, killing every firstborn from every family that didn't have lamb's blood on their doorposts and above their doors.

The Israelites believed Moses, slaughtered a lamb, had a meal, and smeared the lamb's blood as they had been told. That night, every firstborn in Egypt was killed, except for those sleeping in homes with blood on the doorposts, just as Moses had said. When morning came, Pharaoh angrily told Moses to take his people and leave. The Bible says that the next day they packed up everything they owned, along with the things the Egyptians had given them, and headed for what would be known as the Promised Land.

## UNCERTAIN TIMES

Fourteen hundred years later, Jesus was preparing to gather with his disciples for the Passover meal, as they had done before. When they had gathered for previous Passover meals, things had been great. Jesus was a celebrity, a cultural icon, and was drawing thousands of people when he spoke. The disciples felt privileged to be so close to him. The crowds were getting bigger and bigger, as were the miracles.

But this time was different. Things weren't going well. The momentum had turned. Uncertainty was in the air. Rumors were circulating that people were trying to isolate Jesus from the crowds, to get him alone, to falsely accuse him, and to arrest him. The disciples knew that if Jesus went down, they'd go down with him.

On the afternoon of Passover, Jesus still hadn't told them where they would celebrate. Instead, as they headed toward Jerusalem, he told them that things were going to get really bad. Like us, they wondered, *Then why would we go there?* It was as if he had a death wish.

When they arrived on the outskirts of Jerusalem, they waited for the sun to set. Then Jesus sent two of the disciples into town to meet a mysterious man who took them to a secret place. Somehow, Jesus had arranged the Passover meal, but he hadn't told his disciples about it. Because they would be isolated from the crowds and vulnerable, he didn't want anyone to know where they would be. They snuck into Jerusalem under cover of night. They went to a home, slipped quietly upstairs, and gathered in an upper room. It was eerie.

Mark 14:17 – 18 recounts their arrival: "When evening came, Jesus arrived with the Twelve. While they were reclining at the table eating, he said, 'I tell you the truth, one of you will betray me — one who is eating with me.'" That must have seemed odd, even a little insulting. It would be like inviting someone into your home and saying, "Thanks for coming. By the way, I know you're going to betray me." It messed with their minds, and the disciples tried to get Jesus to be more specific, but he only repeated that his betrayer was in the room, adding, "It would be better for him if he had not been born" (v. 21).

Then at this last meal, Jesus began talking about his death, about being taken. The disciples tried to block it out. To their way of thinking — much like our own — if God were with you, then things would get better. When God shows up, there should be more certainty, not less.

Not this time.

## A SOURCE OF COMFORT

Our nation is facing uncertainty like many of us have never experienced in our lifetimes, which makes the Bible the perfect place to turn. The Bible is full of stories that took place in the midst of uncertainty. If you have a favorite Bible story, verse, psalm, or proverb, it probably unfolded during a time of incredible uncertainty. The Bible is not a compilation of stories about wrinkle-free lives. Not everyone lived happily ever after. Each narrative, every passage, the things we draw hope and security from — all of those came from troubled times in the lives of people who discovered that, in the midst of uncertainty, God is still certain.

You may be familiar with the story of Joseph, the son of Jacob, in the Old Testament book of Genesis. Even if you've had your share of sibling rivalry, you've probably never found yourself at the bottom of a well listening to your brothers deciding your fate. Joseph did. Above him, he could hear them debating:

"Should we sell him or kill him?"

"I don't know ... let's sell him."

"No, let's kill him."

But God was with Joseph in the well and eventually placed him in one of the highest positions of authority in Egypt.

You may think you have problems with your teenaged children. In another story in the Old Testament, King David awoke one day to discover that his son had raised an army and was about to invade the capital city to conquer it and replace him. When you read this story, you discover that God was with David in the middle of that trial.

If you were raised in church, then you probably know the story of a Hebrew mother who feared for the life of her baby son. She heard that Pharaoh was going to kill all of the baby boys because there were too many Israelites in the land. Like any mother who loves her son, she would do anything to protect him. So she wrapped up her newborn, placed him in a basket, and shoved him out into the Nile River, probably thinking, *If it's between the crocodiles and the Egyptian butchers, I'll take my chances with the river.* Baby Moses was found, and he became the deliverer of the nation of Israel. When everything else was uncertain in that mother's life, God wasn't.

Moses' story foreshadowed another baby who would be rescued from a similar fate. Mary and Joseph discovered that Herod, jealously responding to the rumor that a baby had been born who would grow up to become the Jewish king, decided to wipe out an entire generation of Jewish boys. As Herod sent troops to murder the baby boys, Mary escaped to, of all places, Egypt, saving her baby, Jesus. Although there was weeping and wailing in the land, God was in the middle of it all. He still had the whole world in his hands.

In every one of these stories, it seems like things had spun out of control, like all the momentum was backward, like all of God's activity had ceased, like the bad guys—the evil kings, the gods of the pagans—had won. But if you read them closely, you'll discover that in the midst of that extraordinary uncertainty, God was there. Every time. If ever there was a time for us to pick up the Bible and read it, it's now.

## BAD NEWS DOESN'T CHANGE TRUTH

Back to the upper room. As they began eating, Jesus told his disciples that the bread they were eating was his body. He was saying that this isn't what you think it is. You've been eating the Passover meal since childhood, but from now on, when you eat it, this is my body. What did he mean? All that death talk again. All that negativity. And they didn't want to hear it. When God's involved, things have to turn around, don't they? Things are supposed to go well, aren't they? God should bring *more* certainty, not less.

Jesus wasn't finished. As they drank the wine, he told them it was his blood "poured out for many," foreshadowing what would happen just hours later when he would be nailed to a cross and die in front of them. And the news from Jesus got worse as he predicted they would disown him. They left that room and headed to the garden of Gethsemane, where he would be arrested.

Peter was thinking, *Enough of this. Enough bad news. That's enough about death, betrayal, and arrest. No way we're going to let that happen.* Because if God is with you and you're the Son of God, this isn't how the story should go. Like us, Peter believed there should be more certainty, more faith, more miracles, more intervention.

And so we ask, Can we maintain faith in God when there's absolutely no evidence of his activity in our lives, in the world? Can we continue to embrace God as our personal heavenly Father? When we experience extraordinary uncertainty in our families, in our jobs, with our children, with our leaders, with the economy — with all of that uncertainty — can we still trust God?

Your answer will determine your response to continuing uncertainty.

If we asked Jesus' disciples months after he was crucified what their darkest moment had been following Jesus and when they had the least hope, I believe they would have answered, "It was when we realized things weren't going to get better, when he promised us things would get worse, when he predicted that one of us would betray him and that all of us would fall away. It was when we saw him arrested and we denied him. It was when he was tried and convicted and we saw him die. It was when we thought we had wasted our time and that God wasn't there."

If we asked them, When do you think God was doing his greatest work? Was it healing the lame guy, healing the blind, or seeing Lazarus step out of his tomb? I believe they would answer, "Actually, it was during those hours when it seemed he was doing the least. In those darkest moments, when it seemed God was inactive, he was actually the most active." Those hours were the epicenter of the salvation of humankind. Those hours are the ones that, for thousands of years, people all over the world have looked back to, rejoicing in God's goodness and grace. But if you had asked the disciples in those moments, they would have said, "Game over. Not a man of God. We wasted our lives."

Again, God's most amazing work often begins in the biggest messes, in times of brokenness. That's a difficult message for Western Christians. Yet it is the story of those who have chosen to follow God and, specifically, for those who have decided to place their faith in Jesus. It's our story, because for many of us, that's been our experience — that God seems to do his most amazing work through broken, hopeless situations. He shows up in ways we would not choose, because we would never allow things to get as bad as they do. We look left. We look right. We look at circumstances. We doubt. That, more than any other time, is when we should turn to the Bible. Its stories — including the story of our salvation — were birthed in times of extraordinary darkness and uncertainty. You may think, That's neat, even a little inspirational. But it's not going to help me get a job. It won't get my kids back in school. It's not going to affect my wife going to work tomorrow to find out whether she gets to keep her job. It won't earn me a commission. It won't change anything about my prodigal son or my prodigal daughter. It doesn't make me well.

All of that is true. Never has there been a time as a pastor or a church leader that I haven't wanted to be able to promise people that their circumstances will improve. But the question for us is, Will we maintain our faith when we can't see his hand? Even though Scripture doesn't change anything in our circumstances, it does allow us to *embrace* uncertainty knowing that God is still in control, that although life is uncertain, God is not. Family may be uncertain, the economy may be uncertain, and the world may seem uncertain, but God is not. Embracing that truth — even if it's just holding on by our fingernails — can keep us from making decisions that further complicate the difficulties we're facing. Knowing that God is certain allows us to go to bed at night at peace, even in the midst of the storm. Knowing that God is certain helps us keep an eye out for things God is doing that may take us by surprise, just as they often took the characters of the Bible by surprise. God is not uncertain. He still has our whole world in his hands.

## SOMEONE WHO'S BEEN THERE

I recently met a man who reaffirmed this very truth for me. My wife, Sandra, and I were in Washington, D.C., for the National Prayer Service. We had heard that we would have the opportunity to meet President Barack Obama. Handlers took us to the basement of the National Cathedral and had us wait there.

As we waited, they lined us up in the order that we were to meet the president. We were spread out down this wide hall. At the end of the hall were four steps leading up to a hallway, which was intersected by another hallway. The president was going to come around the corner, stand at the top of the stairs, and greet us.

As it happened, I was positioned in line behind a man I had just met, Rev. Otis Moss. Rev. Moss was born in Georgia in 1935 and was orphaned when he was sixteen years old. As a young African-American male in Georgia in 1951, he saw the worst that this country had to offer. Yet he placed his faith in Christ as a teenager, and at nineteen years old, he decided to become a preacher.

Through the years, he was able to connect with Dr. Martin Luther King Jr., and he marched with Dr. King in Selma, Alabama, and in Washington, D.C. Rev. Moss was part of a core group of men and women who experienced things that, hopefully, no one in this country will ever have to experience again. He lost a friend. He saw the division of families. He experienced racism and hatred that most of us can't imagine. Yet through all of those circumstances, he maintained his faith.

I asked Rev. Moss as many questions as I could and then just listened. He was standing with his back to the stairs, talking to me, sharing stories, unbelievable history, conversations with Coretta Scott King and others. Suddenly, in midsentence, he stopped talking to me. He turned toward the stairs, kind of staring off into space, and said, "And we know that in all things God works for the good of those who love him." Just like that, he quoted the first half of

Romans 8:28. I couldn't help thinking that the "all things" in this man's life were nothing like my "all things." Rev. Moss had seen and experienced things that many of us never have or ever will.

I was still standing in awed silence when Rev. Moss turned back to me and said, "But Pastor Stanley, sometimes it takes him a while." Almost the instant he said it, a Secret Service contingent appeared from around the corner. There, standing before us, smiling, was the first African-American president of the United States of America.

I couldn't even begin to appreciate the gravity of that moment for Rev. Moss—for all of us, really—as he stepped forward and shook the president's hand. I knew I was about to meet a president, but I had just had a conversation with a saint. Rev. Moss understands, in a way that most of us will never understand, that when life is uncertain, God is not. He still has your family, your personal finances, and all the things that are worrying you to death in his hands. He still has your whole world in his hands.

Of that you can be certain.

# CHAPTER 6

# G O D

# IS ENCOURAGING

## *Rick Bezet*

When I was growing up in southern Louisiana, I hated church. My family was like many who fought at home and on the way to church, only to be told to smile when we got there. God forbid that anyone could see what was really happening at home! And as a child I begged not to have to go to church, all because of a Sunday school teacher. I still freak out when I think about her. Every week she would talk about hell. I didn't know there was so much to say about hell, but she described it like she was born and raised there.

One day in our class, I remember her saying something that surprised me, and I replied, "Golly!" Immediately she turned my direction and screeched, "What did you say, son?" I whispered it again. "Mr. Bezet, don't you know that *golly* is a form of using God's name in vain?" With her long, bony index finger pointed at me she continued berating me in front of the whole class. "Hell is hot, Bezet, don't you ever forget it." And trust me, I haven't.

Unfortunately, too many people think God is like my dear old Sunday school teacher—a harsh, angry, judgmental, finger-pointing tyrant who cannot wait to identify your failures. That's just not who God is. Every story in the Bible points to one divine message: God is *for* you. He wants you to experience the best. He loves you even when you mess up, and he never gets mad at you. And yet so many Christians continue to live under the weight of condemnation and discouragement, but that doesn't come from God. Even if you've done horrible things and your friends have turned their backs on you and your family won't speak to you, you can count on one thing: God will be right there in your corner encouraging you. The whole world might give up on you, but God never will.

## IS THAT GOD SMILING?

There was a point in my early ministry that I considered quitting. I compared myself with people around me who were great speakers, great teachers, and even scholars, and I felt inferior. "How can I be in the ministry if that is the standard?" I wondered. But as I was having these thoughts, I sensed that still, whispering voice of God telling me something that I wrote down in the back of my Bible. "Rick, I just want you to encourage people."

God encouraged me that day, and he wants us not only to encourage others but also to remind them of his encouraging nature. You can be having the worst day of your life. You got in a fight with your wife before you left for work. A subordinate who reports to you catches you in a white lie. You get a ticket for parking in a handicap parking space at lunch. You miss your daughter's tennis match. And your wife is still mad at you when you get home. You're feeling lower than a snake's belly, and God's smile is so big and his hug so inviting and everything about him says, "Do you know how much I love you?"

Noah built that boat for years, despite the ridicule of family and friends and the fact that it was five hundred miles from the sea. How did he do it? God encouraged him. Moses, who once killed a man, had to deliver to the children of Israel the Ten Commandments, which included the words "Thou shall not kill." Not an easy job, but God encouraged him. Gideon and only three hundred soldiers faced a major battle against an enemy whose camels "could no more be counted than the sand on the seashore." God encouraged him with a dream. David was called a "man after God's heart," even after adultery and murder, and God never gave up on him either. Daniel spent time caged up with lions; the Hebrew children stood strong for God and ended up in a fiery furnace. Mary, the mother of Jesus, suffered the shame of having to give birth in a stable. Paul got thrown into prison for serving God. But throughout the Bible, God comes alongside his children whenever they are going through deep waters and encourages them.

God is for you, not against you.

## THROW THE FIRST STONE

If you asked the woman in the Bible who was caught in adultery, she would tell you that it was the religious people, not God, who were angry with her. Unfortunately, that's where many people get their image of Jesus as an angry, condemning tyrant—from church folk. Imagine a woman in your church who got caught up in an affair with a married man. Let's say the married man had a lovely family and his wife volunteered in the church's ministry to parents of special needs children. Let's make it even more outrageous. The woman in question was a single mom and the man, a licensed auto mechanic, had volunteered to go to her apartment complex to fix her car so she could drive to work. She invites him inside to clean up after he fixed her car and she seduces him and ... you get the idea.

Any reasonable person would castigate that woman for seducing a godly husband who was trying to help her. I know it takes two and that both people sinned, but we love to put the blame on someone, and I'm sure you wouldn't have to look very far to find people in that man's church who would put all the blame on that single mom for what happened. Maybe we wouldn't stone her like they did in Bible days, but we'd surely put her in her place.

Not Jesus. He'd stand right beside her and face all of us who were wagging our fingers at her and reminding her how awful she was. After we got all that indignation out, he would finally speak: "Whoever is perfect, go ahead and throw a stone at her."

Think about it. What could be worse than invading someone's marriage by seducing another woman's husband? Having sex with a man who is married and has a family? Even people who are not

Christians recognize this is really bad. Just look at the way the media (and the rest of us) pounces on politicians who get caught in similar scenarios. They're relentless. They keep showing "the confession" and then bring in all these high-minded commentators to let the whole world know what a creep he is.

What does Jesus do? Here's what he actually said to that woman: "I don't condemn you."

Where's the angry, judgmental, finger-pointing God? He doesn't exist. In his place is a Savior who says, "I love you, no matter what. Your mistake doesn't define you. I know you want to do better, and you can. I forgive you, so get back out there and live like the child of a king."

He could have wagged his finger at her. He could have told her, "I'm so ashamed of you." He could have acted as judge and jury and condemned her to death right there. The Pharisees pointed to their law book, which dictated she should be killed right on the spot. But Jesus had another plan. He wanted to restore her and encourage her to stop sinning. People judge and condemn. God encourages.

The Bible doesn't tell us any more about this woman, but I imagine his encouragement changed her life. I can just see her walking past those judgmental Pharisees with a smile on her face, her head held high. She knew what she did was wrong, and she most likely knew that religious law called for her to be stoned to death. Whenever someone sins, they don't need anyone to remind them that what they did was wrong. They already know, and as the crowd taunted her, she probably felt like the worst failure in the world. But Jesus gave her a second chance. He always does. In an instant she went from shame to confidence. That's what encouragement does to a person. It gives you courage, which manifests itself in confidence.

# VIRAL ENCOURAGEMENT

I can't say this with certainty, but I believe the first thing that woman did after she left Jesus was look for someone in her life who needed some encouragement, because that's another thing encouragement does for us. It makes you so grateful that you want to share it with someone else. If I'm really down about something and someone on my staff knows what I'm dealing with and gives me a little pat on the back and a word of encouragement, it not only lifts me up and helps me keep going, but it also makes me more aware of others in my life who may need a similar boost for their spirits. Encouragement is like a virus, infecting those it touches, who in turn spread it to others.

Recently, my pastor friend Dino Rizzo and I had the opportunity to spend some time with the world-renowned evangelist Billy Graham. Just being with this great man of God was encouraging, but what really impressed me is that as we were about to leave, he asked if he could pray for our churches. Here's a guy who has preached to millions all over the world and has prayed for presidents and kings, and he wants to pray for my church? Talk about a huge lift to our spirits. Almost immediately, I asked him if there was anything we could pray about for him, and his answer astounded me: "Pray for me that I will finish the race." I thought to myself, if Billy Graham needs a prayer like that, we're all in trouble. But even though in his twilight years his health was frail, he was still running, still serving God in any way that he could and wanting us to pray for him.

I came away from that meeting thinking this is the way it ought to be. Three men, separated by a couple of generations, but lifting each other up to God in prayer. We were so touched by his desire to pray for us that we wanted to do the same thing for him.

Could you imagine what would happen if Christians became known for their encouragement? If instead of reminding people how bad they are, we looked for ways to encourage them? Think back on everyone you confronted yesterday: the lady behind the Starbucks counter, the custodian cleaning the lobby as you walk into your workplace, that annoying colleague in the next cubicle, your teenage daughter, her boyfriend, that tech-support guy on the phone who can barely speak English, your spouse. Would any of them have benefitted from a kind, uplifting word of encouragement from you?

I heard about a big executive in an advertising agency who eats out at fancy restaurants a lot, and when the server brings the food to his table, he says, "We're about to say a little prayer for our food. Is there anything you would like us to pray for in your life?" Imagine what that does for the server who's used to being ordered around or, worse, ignored. You don't have to look far to find someone who needs encouragement. We walk past them every day.

I don't ever want to be like my old Sunday school teacher. She may have had a heart for God, but her judgmental attitude made me hate church. Fortunately, I was eventually won over by the kindness of other Christians who reflected God's encouraging nature. As a pastor, I've seen too many people come to church burdened with their own guilt, and I know many more who stay away because they think they're not good enough for God. They don't need me to make them feel worse. What they need is to see the same Jesus that the adulterous woman saw. The Jesus who died for them so that they could be free from their guilt. Our lives are the sermons they use to understand what God is like. My prayer for you and for myself is that we will reflect God's encouragement to a lost and hurting world.

# CHAPTER 7

# G O D

# IS FOR YOU

## *John Burke*

"Get your d—hands off me." Megan whirled around to confront whoever had decided to help himself as she walked by. Quickly assessing the drunken state of the whole table, she opted to head back to the bar. Tony, the piano player, was sitting on a bar stool taking a break.

"I hate it right before closing time," Megan ranted as she set her tray of empty glasses on the bar for Jim to take. "Everyone's so f—plastered, they can't see straight."

"Hey, it pays the bills," Tony offered as he finished a beer. "But I know what you mean. I've been in a funk lately, wondering where my life is going."

"You *have* been pretty pissy lately," Jim chimed in from behind the bar. Jim owned Pete's Piano Bar, located on Sixth Street in Austin, the live music capital of the world. It's the younger, Austin version of Bourbon Street, where Austinites go from bar to bar to hear great music, hook up, and party.

"What's the point? I mean, am I going to be eighty, still leading a bunch of drunks in old Billy Joel songs, closing down Sixth Street?" Tony blurted.

"You have a gift, man," Jim said, offering some encouragement. "You know how to get people into it. That's why Pete's is always their last stop. They love the way you get them singing! It's a gift, and it sells drinks!" Jim grinned. "Now, get back to using your gift and sell us some drinks—it's almost closin' time."

## "THOSE PEOPLE"

What happens on Sixth Street would not be condoned or encouraged in any church. We might tend to think the people who hang out there are the farthest from God, and maybe even that God is farthest from them. I'm sure you have a place like that in your city. The place "those people" go, the ones who seem so far from God. These are the ones who seem beyond hope. The lost causes.

But the more I read the Scriptures, the more I realize that God is *for these people*. He's on their side. And in fact, if Jesus had come in our day, this just might have been his favorite place to hang out— Sixth Street! The more I study his life, the more I'm convinced he would have made friends on Sixth Street. I'm almost certain many Sixth Street people would start following him, and it might look a little messy and confusing. Which raises a question: if Jesus hung out on Sixth Street and attracted some followers, what would happen if they came to your church or mine? What message would they get from us? Would they get the message, "God is for you"? Or would they get some other message?

Over the last ten years, I've deliberately interacted with many people like the ones you'd find on Sixth Street in Austin. In fact, the majority of people who attend our church are people who on the outside seem to be far from God. But the reality is that God is never far from them; he is right here on Sixth Street or wherever they live, drawing them to himself. God is a God of mercy and compassion, and he wants people to know he's for them, not against them. But for that to happen in our cities, we have to let things get messy in the church.

Think about it this way: if the average person under forty-five wants to come hang out with you and your friends to explore faith, more than likely one out of three women and men who come will have had an abortion. One out of four women will have been sexually molested, creating huge trust issues and likely struggles with promiscuity. One out of two people will have lived together before marriage and assume that is the wisest way to avoid the pains of divorce. Most will have been sexually active before marriage and will have struggles with pornography, sexual addictions, and affairs. One in five people who come to your church will struggle with alcohol or drug abuse. One out of five people smoke. One out of two marriages eventually will fail. Do the math — there's a good chance most everyone is struggling with something. Not to mention that demographers tell us there are no moral and behavioral differences for the most part between those who claim to be Christians and those who do not.

## THE MESS

We live in a broken and messy world. But how does any of this change? The apostle Paul tells a messy church in Corinth, a city full of substance abuse, sexual struggles, homosexuality, wealth and partying, even relativism, "I planted the seed, Apollos watered it, but God has been making it grow. So neither the one who plants nor the one who waters is anything, but only God, who makes things grow. The one who plants and the one who waters have one purpose, and they will each be rewarded according to their own labor. For we are God's co-workers" (1 Cor. 3:6–9 TNIV). You aren't responsible for making people grow or change or conform. God is responsible for the growth, for changed hearts. But we do have a responsibility as coworkers. As a coworker, your responsibility is the soil. You help create the right soil in which all people *can* grow, and then God causes growth — in you and in others. And soil is simply the environment, the culture. Churches and religious communities have a distinct culture. When someone from Sixth Street walks into your church, what kind of soil will she encounter?

The Bible records many interactions that Jesus had with the religious leaders of his day. And believe it or not, Jesus reserves some of his harshest words not for the thief, the prostitute, or the drunkard but for religious people. The religious leaders of Jesus' day had a derogatory description of him. He was called "the friend of sin-ners." It was meant as an insult, but it was true. Jesus created an environment where moral foul-ups were attracted to him. He was life-giving to them. Somehow they got the message: "God is for you, not against you."

The biggest problem Jesus had with religious people of his day was their pretense; they spawned a culture of inauthenticity before God and people. This was not just a problem with the religious leaders in Jesus' day; it's a problem for many religious groups today. So how can *we* avoid creating the toxic culture of the Pharisees and instead create the soil, the culture, where God can grow us all?

We have to lose the religious pretense and gain mercy. God is merciful. He loves to show mercy to those who deserve condemna-tion. That's why he told Hosea the prophet, "I desire mercy, not sacrifice." But for us to show God's mercy to a sin-stained world, we must allow things to get messy, trusting God to cause growth. The soil of mercy will get your hands dirty. Jesus' ministry was messy, wasn't it? Isn't this what the religious establishment had trouble with — how messy it looked?

The religious leaders of Jesus' day didn't like messy people; they liked people who kept things looking good on the outside, which is why they complained to the disciples, "Why does your teacher eat with tax collectors and 'sinners'?"

Jesus responded, "It is not the healthy who need a doctor, but the sick. But go and learn what this means: 'I desire mercy, not sacrifice.' For I have not come to call the righteous, but sinners" (Matt. 9:11 – 13). The biting sarcasm of this statement often gets overlooked. Who were the "healthy," "righteous" people Jesus addressed? The ones who would soon crucify Jesus! The Pharisees weren't healthy; they were hiding! They weren't righteous; they were full of religious pretense. They were a mess hiding behind religious inauthenticity, which brought Jesus' harshest critique.

Jesus hung out with corrupt tax collectors, former prostitutes, the partying "sinners" of his day. Jesus associated with messy people like the Samaritan woman, who had racked up five divorces and was shacking up with a sixth man. There was no hiding the mess; it got talked about and written about. Jesus doesn't like pretense; he wants the soil of honesty—people who recognize their own brokenness and depend on God to lead them moment by moment. Jesus came for the messy, honest people who desperately need God.

In this letter to the Corinthians, the apostle Paul reminds the church, "Now you are the body of Christ, and each one of you is a part of it" (1 Cor. 12:27). If the church is to be Jesus' body in the world, then whom do we exist for? The messy, sinful, broken, yet honest people who realize they need God in order to become who God intended them to be.

If we're going to create this environment where messy, broken people can come together and let God grow them into the people he intended, we have to become like God, who is merciful. We have to let go of judging by external appearances; it's not the external sacrifices we can give but a heart growing in love and mercy that God wants us to offer to him, because God is a God of mercy.

## LOSING THE PRETENSE

One Sunday at our church, I taught on this subject of creating a culture of authenticity, and I got an email that afternoon from Tia, a woman who attended: "Today for the first time ever I felt like I had found a place to explore spirituality where I would be accepted. Thank you! I hope to be able to talk my husband into trying our church. We both have tattoos and piercings and have always felt uncomfortable in traditional churches. You are just what I've been asking for. P.S. I almost used my work email to send this, but then I thought, why use a mask? This is me."

I glanced at her email address: "browneyedbi." Tia was bisexual. And she had taken me seriously; she wasn't going to hide it from her new church, which valued authenticity. That's messy. Later that month, she invited my wife, Kathy, and me over for dinner. They were a young family in their late twenties with three children, living in a nice neighborhood. After dinner, Tia's husband, Jim, talked with Kathy about how he and Tia had both been into spirituality but not into God, and how they got married in a "haunted house."

Tia told me how much she liked another message I had given on conflict resolution, based on Matthew 18. "I went home that

Sunday," Tia told me, "called my best friend I hadn't talked to in a year, and we patched things up!"

"What caused the rift?" I asked.

"Oh, Jim got Shelly pregnant when the three of us were having sex together," Tia said, as if telling me the weather forecast. I thought she was going to laugh and say, "Just messing with you, Pastor!" But as she continued, I realized she was serious.

"When Shelly found out, she was furious with me, because she felt like I talked her into it — but it wasn't like it was against her will. Still, ever since that nasty fight, we hadn't talked at all in over a year. And now I've apologized, she forgave me, and we're friends again. I really feel like I'm growing spiritually so much!"

My mind was spinning, and I didn't know what to say. "Lord," I prayed, "she's being so authentic and honest. What do I do? Show me how to represent you." His answer came to me in a thought: *mercy.*

As we talked, Tia admitted bisexuality wasn't healthy for her or her family. I asked why she got into it, and what I heard broke my heart.

"Well, I haven't exactly had a pristine sexual past," Tia explained. "I had some really bad experiences with men early on. My parents divorced when I was a baby, and I spent every summer with my biological father, who started sexually molesting me when I was nine."

"Did your mom know?" I said, imagining the horrible confusion this little girl must have felt as her own father preyed upon her.

"Once I turned thirteen, I refused to see my biological father anymore, but I didn't tell Mom why until I was in my twenties. That wasn't the end of it, though," Tia recalled, as I noticed a sadness bleeding through an otherwise hardened exterior. "I was later gang-raped by some of the football team in high school. That probably had some effect."

As Tia continued, suddenly I realized: I'm looking into the eyes of a little girl who learned from an evil world that her only worth was in what she could do sexually for people — male or female. I took a risk and said, "Tia, I think Jesus is trying to draw you close so that he can begin a healing process in your life. He's already working in your life, Tia, and he loves you and wants the best for you!"

Tia said, "I'm good with God, but I'm not sure about Jesus."

I explained that the reason God sent Jesus was so we could know God in a personal way. So we can know *why* he will forgive us and make us clean, no matter what's happened in the past. "He wants a relationship with you, Tia. He's for you, not against you. Do you know that?" I asked.

"That hasn't really been my impression, especially from Christians," Tia quipped.

"Well, Tia, I really believe if you'll stay open and start seeking to understand who he is, you'll find the love you've been looking for."

Tia joined my wife's small group, where they studied the life of Jesus. She heard real-life struggles from other women and shared her own as they helped each other trust Christ. After about a year of questioning and wrestling, Tia was baptized, professing her faith in Jesus, and began an amazing journey out of bisexuality toward healing and wholeness.

## US VERSUS THEM

God's not interested in our conformity to outward standards. God wants to change us into truly loving people who naturally do what's right, and that's something only God can do — God causes the growth. So Jesus is telling us to lose the religious pretense; that's not the soil where people grow. He wants honest, authentic people who depend daily on God, not people who pretend they are perfect.

Do you feel like you have to pretend around the church? Do you hide the way you usually act in order to fit in at church? External conformity is not God's way. Jesus wants us all to be real, warts and all. Then we can show God's mercy to each other and help each other grow into more of what God intends. God is merciful, and God is for us. Can we show that to others?

Jesus showed mercy to messy people. If they are to become his church today, those of us who *are* his church must lose the "us-them" distinctions. Just notice sometime how often groups of Christians talk about "us," who are in the church, and "them," who are far from God. Notice the culture that describes "them" in ways that come across comparative, disparaging, or like "we" are against "them."

Jesus rebukes unmerciful religious people with this parable: "To some who were confident of their own righteousness and looked down on everyone else, Jesus told this parable: 'Two men went up to the temple to pray, one a Pharisee and the other a tax collector. The Pharisee stood by himself and prayed: "God, I thank you that I am not like other people—robbers, evildoers, adulterers—or even like this tax collector. I fast twice a week and give a tenth of all I get." But the tax collector stood at a distance. He would not even look up to heaven, but beat his breast and said, "God, have mercy on me, a sinner." I tell you that this [tax collector], rather than the other, went home justified before God'" (Luke 18:9–14 TNIV).

You see what Jesus is saying? There aren't two categories of people: "us, who are good" and "them, who are bad." There are just people. All of us desperately need God's mercy, grace, and power to become who God intended us to be. Stop looking at others or treating others as if God is not for them until they change; no one can do that in their own power. God causes the growth.

But God grows all people in the soil of authenticity. We must lose the us-them attitude that judges others but won't lift a finger to help them experience God's love and mercy. Instead of focusing on the external, messy behaviors of others, we must focus on helping them see what God sees in them that was worth dying for. Consider what potential God sees in every created human being: "God saved you by his grace when you believed. And you can't take credit for this; it is a gift from God.... For we are God's masterpiece. He has created us anew in Christ Jesus, so that we can do the good things he planned for us long ago" (Eph. 2:8–10 NLT).

# GOD'S MASTERPIECE

Jesus gave his life so that every willing person could be restored into right relatedness with God by grace. He did it *so that* we would all let God lead us daily to become the masterpiece he intended. What if we created a culture focused on calling out the masterpiece God sees waiting to be revealed in Christ?

If you found a Rembrandt painting covered in mud, you wouldn't focus on the mud or treat it like mud. Your primary concern would not be the mud at all, though it would need to be removed. You'd be ecstatic to have something so valuable in your care. I'll bet you wouldn't try to clean it up by yourself, for fear you might damage it. You would carefully bring this work of art to a master, who could guide you in how to restore it to the condition originally intended.

When people begin treating one another as God's masterpieces waiting to be revealed, God's grace grows in their lives and cleanses them. What do you see first in others — the mud or the masterpiece? Jesus says lose the us-them distinction that focuses on the mud first. Instead, point out the masterpiece in one another and encourage each other to submit to the Master's restoration process — that's the soil in which God grows us all.

And since all of us are works of art in progress, we must lose the need to pretend we're perfect. Jesus said, "Woe to you, teachers of the law and Pharisees, you hypocrites! You clean the outside of the cup and dish, but inside they are full of greed and self-indulgence. Blind Pharisee! First clean the inside of the cup and dish, and then the outside also will be clean" (Matt. 23:25 – 26 TNIV).

Jesus never condoned wrong behavior. Instead, he showed people a more fulfilling way to live, connected moment by moment to the God who gives life. That's why messed-up, imperfect people were attracted to him. They were never in danger of pretending they were perfect, so they were open to admitting their wrongs and depending on God.

So Jesus gets in the face of the religious leaders. The people who worked their whole lives to prove to everyone that they were okay were uncovered. The truth is they still struggled. They still had self-centered, greedy tendencies, secret struggles they hid from others, but God knows the heart. I think Jesus is saying, "Lose the need to pretend you are perfect" — no perfect people allowed in his church.

Nobody's perfect, nobody's sin-free, nobody's untarnished. And the only way to grow into the masterpiece God intended is if we create a confessing culture. We must create the soil where it's safe to be ourselves, warts and all, and instead of judgment and condemnation, we receive mercy and grace and prayer for our struggles. That's why Jesus' half-brother James says, "Therefore confess your sins to each other and pray for each other so that you may be healed" (James 5:16 TNIV).

God heals us all as we create the environment, the soil, where it's okay to confess sins, failures, and struggles. The only way we will do this is if there's mercy and grace, if we remind each other that "God is for us, not against us; and I'm for you!" Then we're not alone in our struggles; God is with us, and we are standing with each other in his mercy and grace, trusting him more. In that environment, God heals us and grows us all.

This is what all people long for. It's what the world is dying for—a place where we can fully be ourselves; a place where authentic strugglers will not be judged and rejected but instead find mercy and help to become more, because God is for us, for all of us, including those on Sixth Street.

Remember Tony, who led drunken sing-alongs for years on Sixth Street? He lived a pretty rough life that eventually caught up with him. He describes his journey toward meeting God:

> I had come to the end of myself. I had reached a point of a lot of emptiness. My career was empty. I had a lot of bottled-up anger. I had this big hole inside of me. My boss (the bar owner) told me about our church in a deep conversation one night. He had never been to Gateway but had heard it was for people like us. When I came semi-exploring faith, my life was pretty messy. I didn't know it was wrong to sleep with your girlfriend before marriage; I just didn't know. But I didn't feel judged or like my sexual sin or my bar job was the central issue. I felt a warm environment that made me feel like people were honestly glad I was there, and it made me want to discover more about their God.
>
> J. J., Gateway's music director, took interest in me and would tell me things he saw God doing in me, long before I could see it. The more I learned, and the more I brought my stuff out with God and others, the more God met me and healed some of the anger-laced wounds. As I learned to daily follow Christ, he took some of the desires away that were not his will and replaced them with new desires.

Tony not only came to faith at our church, he led his waitress friend to Christ and helped baptize her. Tony is now using his gift not to sell drinks but as the worship leader for our church, helping others experience God's mercy and grace.

But it didn't start in our church; it started on Sixth Street, where Jesus still hangs out today.

# CHAPTER 8

# G O D

# IS PRESENT

*Perry Noble*

I don't like to be away from my family, but sometimes I am invited to other churches and conferences to speak, which means I occasionally have to travel. I know some people love to travel, but I'm not one of them. For one thing, planes seem to be built for people who are under four feet tall, and well, I'm a big guy. Sitting all scrunched up in that tiny little seat is bad enough, but when the guy in front of me tries to turn his seat into a La-Z-Boy recliner, let's just say I am less than happy. But the main reason I'm not a big fan of travel is that I miss my family so much when I'm away from them.

Thankfully, my wife, Lucretia, knows how much I dislike being away from them, so when I travel, she always tries to meet me at the church to see me off, and I've got to tell you, that makes all the difference. If I have a really early flight, I at least get a nice "I love you" as she rolls back to sleep, and that's great. But if my flight is later in the day, she and my daughter, Charisse, meet me at the church with hugs and kisses. I love that.

One morning while I was getting ready to leave our house, Lucretia asked me what time I was going to leave the church to go to the airport. I told her we would probably leave around 11:00

a.m., and I was pumped when she said that she and Charisse would be able to meet me there before I left. I grabbed my bag and headed out the door, really looking forward to seeing her and Charisse again before I went to the airport.

I got to the office and it was already one of those days. My phone was ringing, my in-box was full, and my staff was asking my opinion on millions of things. I had to make a ton of quick decisions, and I barely had time to think. It was one of the busiest, craziest, most frustrating mornings I have ever had in the office. Around 10:45 I was about to go nuts, so I told everyone going on the trip with me to get their luggage and head for the car. We had been driving for about fifteen minutes when my phone rang. It was Lucretia.

"Where *are* you?"

That's when it hit me. She was at the church, waiting to say goodbye to me, and I had already left. I was here, she was there, and it felt like we were a million miles apart, thanks to my being in such a hurry. I had forgotten that my dear wife and little girl had planned to stop by the church and see me off—something I normally cherish. But I had gotten so caught up in all that was going on at the office and the frustration it produced that I forgot something incredibly important to me. Not only did I feel like a jerk, I felt terribly alone.

Jesus' last words are in Matthew 28:20. He said, "And surely I am with you always, to the very end of the age." I think many times in our busy lives it's easy to do with God what I did with my wife: forget him. I love nothing more than being with my wife and having her encourage me as I'm about to leave home. But I let the chaos of a busy morning at the office get in the way of the very thing I cherished the most.

Jesus' words give us comfort because we know they are a promise to all of us who are his followers. But then we get caught up in the busyness of our lives and forget them. We go about our lives as if he is someplace far away and we're on our own. Is it any wonder we sometimes feel that God has abandoned us? Just as I missed the encouraging hug of my wife and daughter, we often forget that God is right there beside us wherever we go. No matter where we are, God is present.

# THE WORD *IS* GOD

I know it's hard sometimes to feel God's presence, but he is actually here with us. I believe if we, as followers of Christ, could wrap our minds around that concept, it would revolutionize the way we approach our lives.

The Bible gives us four accounts of the life of Jesus in the Gospels. When we feel like we are alone, we can read about Jesus and his life. Jesus left heaven to come here. I've heard people say the only reason Jesus came to earth was to die for our sins. If that were true, why did it take him thirty-three years to do it?

Jesus came to earth to pay for our sins, but I believe he lived here for thirty-three years to model for us how we should live life. Jesus tells us in John 5:30, "By myself I can do nothing." One of the reasons we struggle so much is because we're trying to do things by ourselves. Jesus is telling us we can't do anything without him. I believe if we make it our goal to keep our eyes on Jesus and live a life that pleases him, it makes it really hard to forget he is with us.

Although God is present wherever we are, it is so easy to get wrapped around our daily schedules that we forget about him. That's why finding a time each day to spend in prayer and reading the Bible is so important for us. When I am alone and it's quiet and I open my Bible and begin reading, I know that God is right there with me, speaking to me through his Word.

If you feel distant from God, meet him in his Word.

# NO LONGER SEPARATED

One of the things I have seen in my years as a pastor is that some people feel distant from God because they are still carrying around guilt from their past. Even though they have been forgiven, they live more like convicted criminals than redeemed children of God. While it is true that our sins separated us from God, it is also true that his grace covered those sins and brought us back into a personal relationship with him.

Jesus took your punishment for your sins so that you don't have to. You don't have to work to become "good enough" to enjoy God's presence. His death on the cross made you good enough, and he wants nothing more than to be with you forever. The apostle Paul explains in 2 Corinthians 5:21 that "God made him who had no sin to be sin for us, so that in him we might become the righteousness of God." The Bible tells us that our sins are no longer held against us and that God has cleaned up our mess and removed it "as far as the east is from the west."

Because of Jesus' death and resurrection, we are no longer separated from him. Whenever you think your sins are too great to allow you to have a relationship with God, think about this: "Who shall separate us from the love of Christ? Shall trouble or hardship or persecution or famine or nakedness or danger or sword?... No, in all things we are more than conquerors through him who loved us. For I am convinced that neither death nor life, neither angels nor demons, neither the present nor the future, nor any powers, neither height nor depth, nor anything else in all creation, will be able to separate us from the love of God that is in Christ Jesus our Lord" (Rom. 8:35 – 39).

Who or what you used to be no longer matters. Jesus came so that he could be with you. The death of Jesus is a reminder that he is with us. Forever.

## RUNNING UP THE SCORE

I have a confession to make: I am a video-game junkie. I especially love playing sports video games. I love to beat people and really run up the score. If you ever want to play me, I have to warn you: I have no mercy. I'm not the kind of guy who feels sorry for the opponent who gets behind. I go for the win.

I'm not sure why winning is so much fun, but it is. After I waste an opponent, I get a small taste of what it might be like to be in the locker room of the winning team after the Super Bowl. The champagne showers. Everyone laughing and high-fiving each other. The only word I can think of to describe those scenes is *exhilarating*.

And then, the cameras always give us a small peek into the locker room of the losing team, and it's almost like a funeral. Blank stares. Guys just sitting there wondering what happened. Even a few tears from big guys who don't normally cry.

A lot of times, Christians act like the guys in the losing locker room when we should be partying with the winners. We forget that as followers of Jesus we are on the winning team: "He gives us the victory through our Lord Jesus Christ" (1 Cor. 15:57). It's a lot easier to feel God's continual presence when you know you are on the winning team and will someday be with him in heaven forever.

Sometimes in life it doesn't always feel like you're on the winning team. You may have received a bad diagnosis from your doctor or you may have lost a good job that you had for twenty years, but as a follower of Jesus, you win. The victory has already been won, and even in the midst of life's trials, you can celebrate as a winner.

Two thousand years ago on a Friday, it all seemed to be coming apart for Jesus. His disciples abandoned him and he was being beaten and murdered. It seemed like God was out of control, but he used those very circumstances to prove to the world that he was and is in control. Many of us may feel like it's Friday and we're being crucified, but Sunday is coming, and God will get all the glory. The same power that conquered the grave lives in every believer. We all have the victory of Jesus inside of us. If we walk in that victory, rather than thinking we are fighting for victory, we'll understand he's present in our lives.

# CHAPTER 9

# G O D

## IS ABLE

### *Jentezen Franklin*

Five kings were keeping God's people from entering the Promised Land. Joshua and his army chased them, so they hid in a cave. Joshua had some of his men block the entrance to the cave, trapping the kings inside while the rest of his army slaughtered the kings' forces. Once the battle was over, Joshua told the soldiers guarding the entrance to the cave to bring the five kings to him. Here's what happened next: "And it came to pass, when they brought out those kings unto Joshua, that Joshua called for all the men of Israel, and said unto the captains of the men of war which went with him, Come near, put your feet upon the necks of these kings. And they came near, and put their feet upon the necks of them. And Joshua said unto them, Fear not, nor be dismayed, be strong and of good courage: for thus shall the LORD do to all your enemies against whom ye fight. And afterward Joshua smote them, and slew them, and hanged them on five trees" (Josh. 10:24–26 KJV).

This King James Version of the story uses a word that we don't use that much: *dismayed*. Its most literal translation is "to be made unable." So Joshua was saying to his men, "Don't be made unable. Don't fall apart. Don't freak out. Even though you're facing impossibility, a great opposition, don't be afraid. Your God is able, but first you have to get victory over these five kings."

God is still able, but first you have to kill five kings, and I like to think of those kings as our five senses. If you're going to win the battle of faith—if you're going to see your family blessed, see your life blessed, see God's favor—then you have to overcome these five kings. Your five senses—what you can smell, what you can feel, what you can see, what you can hear, and what you can taste—are powerful evangelists of unbelief. If you allow them to, your five senses can talk you out of what God's Word has promised you. You have to learn to put your foot on the necks of your five senses. You have to subdue them and say, "You're not going to steal from me what I know God's Word has promised me."

## THE SMELL OF TRUTH

In Daniel 3, Shadrach, Meshach, and Abednego were thrown into the fiery furnace. When God brought them out, not a hair on their heads was burned. Scripture makes an interesting distinction: "there was no *smell* of fire on them" (emphasis mine). In other words, they went through a fiery situation where they *should* have been burned, but they came through without even the smell of smoke.

God doesn't want you to go through fiery trials and smell like them for the rest of your life. Sometimes I meet people who have been through a fiery trial, and every time I'm around them, that's all they can talk about. Maybe you were burned in a relationship. Maybe you were burned in a business deal. Maybe you were burned at a church because some preacher was a hypocrite or somebody hurt you. Perhaps now you judge everybody the same way. If you're going to win your faith fight, first you have to gain victory over what you smell.

I don't want to smell like everything I've been through. Ministry has taken me through a lot of stuff. People in ministry can take home the smell of their work. We deal with problems and lots of messy issues, but I don't want to take that smell home to my kids. Just imagine how those Old Testament priests must have smelled: the blood, the gore, the burning of sacrifices. That's why the priests had to burn incense. God said, "To kill the smell of ministry, burn incense." Worship is a type of burning incense. Worshiping helps grant us victory over smell.

In John 11, Lazarus had been dead for four days when Jesus told them to take the stone away from the front of his grave. When Martha said, "Lord, by this time he stinketh," that was a statement of unbelief. Jesus had already told them they were going to see God's glory. Jesus didn't care what condition Lazarus was in. Jesus was suggesting to them, "Even if it stinks, still believe."

Maybe your marriage stinks, but still believe. Maybe your finances stink right now, but still believe. Maybe your children are going through a season in which it seems like they just can't get their act together and you feel like giving up. In spite of what you smell, in spite of what you feel, in spite of what you see, in spite of what you hear, in spite of what you taste, you have to realize that our God is able. If you're going to conquer, you have to get your foot on your sense of smell.

I heard a story about some children who played a trick on their grandpa. He had one of those long handlebar mustaches. He was taking a nap, and these little brats snuck in and rubbed some limburger cheese on his moustache. When he woke up, he said, "Whew! This bedroom stinks." He went to the kitchen and still smelled it, so he said, "Wow, this kitchen stinks too." Then he stepped outside into his back yard and said, "Man, the whole world stinks!" If you're not careful, if you get burned by enough people, you might start going around with an old stinky attitude and old stinky words. Even though you've been through the fire, you don't have to smell like it. Burn some incense of praise and thank God you still have a future.

## FEEL FREE

The second king we have to get our foot on is the sense of what we feel. If you don't master your feelings, you'll start to trust them more than your faith. Jeremiah 17:9 says, "The heart is deceitful above all things." Your feelings are a true enemy of your faith.

Isaac had gone blind in his old age and was on his deathbed when his son Jacob came to him covered with goat hair with the intent to deceive him. Jacob's brother, Esau, was a hairy man, and Jacob had come to steal his birthright.

His blind daddy asked, "Who is it?"

Jacob said, "It's me, Dad. It's your oldest son, Esau. I've come for my blessing from you."

Scripture tells us that the old man reached up and started feeling his arm, trying to determine whether it was his oldest, hairy boy. Isaac said, "You *sound* like Jacob, but you *feel* like Esau." Isaac decided to go with his feelings, rather than with what he was hearing. As a consequence, he gave his blessing to the wrong son. If we go by what we feel instead of what we hear from God's Word, we will miss the truth every time. We have to get past our feelings.

Your feelings are fickle. Sometimes in church you get your feelings hurt. Sometimes in ministry you get your feelings hurt. Sometimes in marriage you absolutely will get your feelings hurt. We have to learn how to subdue our feelings. We have to put our foot on the neck of our feelings and say, "I can't let my feelings stop me. Just because I didn't get the solo on the praise team, I'm not going to quit the praise team. Just because my pastor gave this job to that person instead of to me, I'm not going to let my feelings get so hurt that I stop working for the kingdom. I'm not working for my pastor; I'm working for Jesus." We have to get victory over our feelings.

In the story of Noah's ark, thousands of animals are all thrown in together, natural predators of one another. Yet you don't read of a single fight breaking out on that ark. I believe the last command God gave Noah before he shut the door on the ark was, "Keep the woodpeckers above the waterline." Every church, every ministry, every business has woodpeckers. These are the troublemakers who get below the waterline and just start pecking away, determined to sink the whole thing. Most often, it's because they've had their feelings hurt. We can't allow our feelings to stop us from doing what God has called us to do. Step on the neck of King Feeling and keep going. If you don't, you're going to live a life of defeat.

## MAKE COVENANT WITH YOUR EYES

The Old Testament tells us in 2 Kings 6 a really interesting story about Elisha the prophet and his servant. The king of Aram was at war with Israel, and he had it in for Elisha because God kept telling

Elisha the king's plans in advance. So at one point, Elisha and his servant were in a city surrounded by enemy soldiers. Elisha sent his servant out to assess the situation. When he realized they were surrounded, Elisha's servant returned, almost in a panic. He said, "Oh, my lord, what shall we do?" Elisha told him, "Don't be afraid," and he prayed over him, "Lord, open his eyes so he may see." When his servant went back out, he didn't just see ground level anymore. Now he could see the armies of God, "the hills full of horses and chariots of fire all around Elisha."

Our problem is the same as Elisha's servant: when we get in a battle, all we see is ground level. But as believers, we're supposed to lift up our eyes to the hills, where our help comes from. Our help comes from the Lord, Maker of heaven and earth (Ps. 121:1–2). When you get a bad report, when you get a bad X-ray, when something happens in your family that pits you against an impossibility, when you're facing a difficulty that seems too big for you to overcome, you see to talk you out of what God has promised you. Ultimately, God has promised you victory in your life. Paul says in Philippians 1:21, "For to me, to live is Christ and to die is gain." Even in death, we can be victorious.

I don't know what you're seeing. You may see only your enemy. Then you should pray. If you'll look through faith, you won't see just the enemy; you can see angels. You don't have to see only problems; you can see promises. You have to choose: what are you going to focus on? Are you going to focus on the problem? Or are you going to focus on the promise? What are you looking at? What are you seeing? What are you focusing on? God's Word is just as real as the bad report.

I heard about a chicken yard with a big hen house, where a rooster had all of his hens laying eggs. One day, two little boys were next door playing football, with a brand new white football. One of them accidentally kicked the football over the fence, and it rolled into the chicken yard. The rooster walked around and around the football, examining it carefully. Finally, he called out to all of his hens, "Come on out here, ladies!" When they had all gathered around, he said, "Now, girls, I don't mean to be negative, but here's the kind of eggs they're producing next door. You need to step up your efforts."

We can easily look with our eyes at someone else's life, someone else's success, and envy what they have. What we should be doing instead is focusing on the blessings that God has already given us. Get your foot on what you see and say, "Lord, I believe what you said is true." Don't let circumstances talk you out of your miracle.

A couple of years ago, God gave our ministry, which is based in Georgia, the vision to start holding services in Orange County, California. When I flew out there for our first service, about a hundred people showed up, when we were expecting a thousand. I was pretty discouraged.

I had to start fighting that king of what I could see. We didn't feel that God was sending us to Orange County for a little thing. We really believed that he was sending us out there to reach a mighty harvest. I had to constantly put my foot on the neck of what I could see, and on the neck of what I could feel. There were Sundays when I would preach two times in Georgia and then hop on a plane, even when I didn't feel like going to California. But we knew God had told us to go, so we kept going. I'd walk in, we'd start putting chairs out, and sometimes I'd be thinking, *Is anybody even going to come?* But you can't go by what you see. You have to do what God tells you to. After a year, almost two thousand people were coming regularly. God is faithful. He's able.

## DO YOU HEAR WHAT I HEAR?

Be careful what you listen to. In Mark 4:24 (KJV), Jesus said, "Take heed what ye hear." Be careful what you allow to cross that bridge of your ear into your spirit, because it can contaminate your faith.

In the Old Testament, there's a story about Elijah where everybody is saying recession, everybody's saying poverty, everybody's saying famine, everybody's saying layoffs, and everybody's saying how bad things are. And on top of that, you're probably going to catch swine flu too. "You're going to lose your job, you're going to get swine flu, you're going to lose everything, you're not going to make it." Right in the middle of all those bad reports—ABC, NBC, Woe-Is-Me-TV—the prophet Elijah said, "I hear the sound of an abundance of rain" (see 1 Kings 18:41).

I'm of course talking about faith. Many believers will just join in with the negative spirit of the world. That can't be us. We have to put our foot on what hear, even when we keep hearing it every day. Elijah could hear something different than everybody else. He was tuned in to a different frequency. It's not mind over matter; it's faith over unbelief. Believe God's Word and what he says over what everybody else says. Stop caring what everybody else says. Listen really closely, until you can hear the sound of an abundance of rain.

In 2 Samuel 5:22–24, David was about to go into battle against the Philistines. When he inquired of the Lord about what he should do, God answered him, "As soon as you hear the sound of marching in the tops of the balsam trees, move quickly, because that will mean the LORD has gone out in front of you to strike the Philistine army." David listened, and he was victorious. I don't know what you're hearing, but I hear a sound like marching in the tops of the trees. I hear the sound of victory coming.

I hear the sound of blessing coming. I hear the sound of favor coming. I hear the sound of healing coming. I hear the sound of blessed children rising up, serving Christ. People may say things to me like, "Your kids are just going to be rebellious. That's the reality of the world we live in today." I won't listen to that. I will believe God's report. As believers, we're not to allow our enemy to overtake us with his words. We must not succumb to his lies.

When we get victory over our hearing, we tune in to the Lord's report. We choose to believe what he says. Some might say, "Well, you don't know what kind of bad news I have." It doesn't matter. Our God is able, in spite of what you hear.

## THE TASTE OF VICTORY

There's a story in the Old Testament, in 2 Kings 4:38–42, about a pot of stew during a famine. As the men in the story began to eat it, they discovered that it had accidentally been poisoned. Elisha told them to put flour, or meal, into the pot, and it saved them. I believe that this meal represents the bread of life, which is the Word of God. Whatever is poison in your life, put some Word in it. Is your marriage poisoned? Put some meal in the stew. Are your children making poor choices? Start praying back to God the things that God has already promised you in his Word.

Faith places no limitations on God, and God places no limitations on faith. Take the bread of God's Word, the meal, and put it into your poison. Instead of getting up every day and saying, "I don't know why I'm even going to work today. I know I'm not going to sell anything anyway," put some Scriptures into your poisonous situation. Get victory over your sense of taste.

As Jesus was hanging on the cross, some of the people there attempted to give him a sponge dipped in vinegar and gall. Vinegar and gall has an extreme, bitter taste. I believe this symbolizes for us that they wanted Jesus to become bitter because of what they were doing to him. But Scripture says that Jesus refused to drink the bitter sponge they were offering him. At that moment, Jesus got victory over the fifth king. Although they had hurt him, had wronged him, had inflicted incredible pain on him, he knew he was innocent. His actions essentially said, "I refuse to become bitter."

You may have been wronged. You may have been hurt. To live victoriously in this life, you need to put your foot on that situation. Satan intends it to make you bitter, to make you angry, to make you upset, tense, messed up, and angry. But put your foot on its neck. Tell the king of the sense of taste, "I refuse to take in bitterness. The power of Christ lives in me, so I can forgive. I can love my enemies. I can do good to those who have wronged me." That's the power of a life filled with faith.

## DO MORE THAN OVERCOME

A guy came to my church once and preached a message on David and Goliath. As you might imagine, I've heard some great sermons on David and Goliath. But this guy focused on why David picked up five stones. He proved biblically that Goliath had four brothers. He suggested that it was David's intention to wipe out Goliath's whole family. The five stones were David saying, "I'm not just going to kill Goliath, but if his brothers want to pick a fight, bring 'em on."

Makes sense to me.

I heard another man preach on the five stones, and he said, "The five stones represent the letters in the name of him who would bring deliverance from the Goliath of sin: J-E-S-U-S." That's a good message too. (All you need is a Hammond organ and a Pentecostal crowd, and you could have church.)

Do you know why I think David picked up four more stones than he needed? I think it was because he was afraid he might miss. It doesn't take a *lot* of faith; it only takes faith the size of a mustard seed—just a *little* faith. You don't have to have great faith, just a *little* faith. One day as I read about David picking up five stones, I felt like the Lord was speaking to me, saying, "Son, always remember: I'll never send you into battle against a great, gigantic problem where I'll give you only *enough* to defeat him. I'll give you *more* than enough. One stone would be enough, but I'll give you more than enough."

God is able, but first you have to kill those five kings that are keeping you out of the Promised Land. He's already given you more than enough to defeat them.

# CHAPTER 10

# G O D

# IS IN CONTROL

*Greg Surratt*

On December 30, 2000, a deranged man broke into the cockpit of British Airways flight 2069 bound for Nairobi, Kenya. He grabbed the controls from the pilot and plunged the Boeing 747 jumbo jet into a steep dive. As the plane fell several thousand feet, dozens of passengers were thrown upward from their seats, hitting their heads on the plane's ceiling. One passenger said the rapid descent felt like being on a giant roller coaster. At first, people screamed as the plane veered sharply to the left and then headed nose down toward the ocean below. Then it got real quiet.

"The plane was really out of control," recounted passenger Zane Augur, an American businessman. (Source: Ian Fisher, "Pilots Avert Crash of British Jet After Attacker Is Subdued," *New York Times*, December 30, 2000.)

Fortunately, the pilot regained control and flew on safely to Nairobi.

I wasn't on that plane, but I know what it feels like to lose control. Have you ever driven on an icy road and your car starts to slide sideways and no matter what you do, you can't get it straightened out? You're out of control, and if you're lucky, you'll just end up in a ditch.

Many interstate highways in mountain states like Colorado have "runoff zones" at the bottom of steep inclines for trucks and other vehicles whose brakes fail. I've never seen one being used, but I'll bet it's pretty scary for the driver to be holding onto the wheel of a forty thousand pound vehicle that's out of control.

Sometimes, our lives feel as if they're spinning out of control. I love the tagline of an insurance commercial: "Life comes at you fast." I never thought I'd say things like, "Seems just like yesterday," but that's how fast it's been, and most of the time I've felt like that guy who spins plates on top of those long sticks and keeps running back and forth trying to keep the plates spinning.

Most of us like to be in control, some so much that we have a name for them: control freaks. But all of us like to control things to a certain extent: our finances, our relationships, our tempers, our appetites. Control is good, but sometimes life is like that Boeing 747 in a freefall toward the ocean. In fact, most things in life are outside of your control. You walk into your office one day and discover your job has been eliminated. You never saw it coming, and even if you did, you had no control over it. Or you get one of those frantic phone calls from your wife. There's been an accident. Talk about feeling out of control.

Because we like to be in control, these out-of-control moments are unsettling. The temptation is to let that situation control you. I know people who have been immobilized by an unexpected event in their lives. It overshadows everything, making it difficult for them to function normally. I would love to tell you that as followers of Christ you will never have any of those out-of-control situations, but if I did, I would be lying. The Bible says that the rain falls on the just and the unjust, meaning life happens. To everyone. But the hope I *can* give you is this: even when things seem to be spinning out of control in your life, God is still in control. Nothing unexpected happens with God. Whatever out-of-control moment you are going through, God has chosen you to experience it, and he has a plan for you to get through it.

## GOD HAS CHOSEN YOU

Do you remember a time in your life when you were really excited about being chosen for something that was important to you? It may have been when sides were picked for a sandlot baseball game, or when you were selected to lead a team at work. Someone chose you for a special reason, and it felt great, didn't it? In fact, it may have changed the way you thought about yourself and your future, at least for that season of your life.

When I entered the seventh grade, my family had moved into a new neighborhood, so I became the new kid in school. To make matters worse, I was a nerd before nerds were cool. Long hair and jeans were the style then, but I sported a flattop haircut and wore JC Penney double knit pants. It was the perfect storm of social awkwardness.

Shortly after the school year started, I learned that we would be having a dance, but not an ordinary dance. We were having a Sadie Hawkins Day dance. I'm not sure they still do that; in fact, it might not even be politically correct. Sadie Hawkins was a fictional character in an old cartoon strip called *Li'l Abner*. She was described as the "homeliest gal in all them hills," so her father had to come up with a plan to find her a husband. He picked out a day and called it Sadie Hawkins Day and sponsored a race for all the bachelors in town. They got a head start and then Sadie began chasing them. Whoever got caught had to marry her.

At our Sadie Hawkins Day dance, the girls had to ask the boys to the dance, which was unwelcome news to me because (1) I knew no girl would choose me and (2) even if someone was that desperate, I wouldn't be able to go. My father was a pastor and our little church had a rather strict code of conduct. Dancing was definitely on the list of things we didn't do.

As luck would have it, a pretty girl chose me! All of the sudden I felt like the coolest guy in school, even with my flattop and double knits. It didn't matter anymore that I was the new kid—something I had no control over and didn't particularly like. I was so excited, I snuck to the dance despite my dad's restrictions. (Some things are worth taking a licking for!)

When things begin to spin out of control and you feel like a tiny little cog in a giant wheel, stop for a moment and remember that God is in complete control, even if you're not. He chose you before he created the world and knows exactly what you are going through.

According to the Bible, he adopted us as his sons and daughters "in accordance with his pleasure and will" (Eph. 1:5). Your out-of-control moment is all a part of his sovereign will to make you more like his Son, Jesus.

When that girl chose me, it was to go to the dance. I was history to her after that. When God chooses you, he adopts you, makes you a part of his family. Although I haven't had any personal experience with adoption, I've known couples who have adopted children, and it's such a beautiful act. The closest thing to adoption I've experienced is the addition of four new family members when my four kids got married. They really are like part of the family, and that's what happens when God chooses you. Almost.

You see, I didn't choose these new family members. My kids did, and if you asked them, they would probably say they chose the smartest, best-looking, near-perfect individuals on earth, and I wouldn't disagree. They're just plain neat people; they *deserved* to be chosen.

Not you. Not any of us. The Bible says we are all impure and infected with sin (Isa. 64:6 NLT). God knew that but he chose you anyway. Imagine a criminal standing before a wise judge. After declaring the criminal guilty and sentencing him to death, the judge removes his robe, walks over to the shameful criminal, and says, "Even though you are guilty as charged, I am going to pay your penalty, and if you'll just sign these adoption papers here, you will be a part of my family, live in my home, take on my name and reputation, and have access to my resources."

God has chosen you, in spite of you. You didn't deserve it, but he chose you anyway. He knows who you are and what you've done, and he still chose you. Because you are part of his family, nothing is out of control. You may not be in control of your circumstances right now, but you can take comfort in the knowledge that the God who chose you before he created the world is in complete control of your life.

# GOD HAS PLANNED FOR YOU

When things spin out of control in our lives, it feels as if God has forgotten us. We like to give him credit when everything is going according to plan, but when something unexpected comes along and turns our world upside down, we wonder why he abandoned us. But according to the Bible, God never leaves us or forsakes us (Deut. 31:6). God is consistent. He does not work part time. He is in control every minute of the day, and whatever you are going through is part of his perfect plan.

The apostle Paul put it this way: "In him we were also chosen, having been predestined according to the plan of him who works out everything in conformity with the purpose of his will, in order that we, who were the first to hope in Christ, might be for the praise of his glory" (Eph. 1:11 – 12).

People sometimes become uneasy about words like *predestined*, *chosen*, *election*, and *foreknowledge*, but all this is saying is that God is in control. He has a plan and a purpose, and he has given you the blessed opportunity to be a part of that plan. You may not see that purpose when things seem to be out of control. But it's there. God has a divine reason for your out-of-control moments. What seems like chaos and confusion now will make sense later, if not in your lifetime, then when you receive your reward in heaven. The "bad things" that happen to us are part of the "everything" he works out as part of his plan.

A few years ago, our church had grown to the point where we had to enlarge our facilities. At the time, we were conducting five weekend services to accommodate our growth, and we had run out of room for children's and other ministries. We began the tedious process of selecting an architect and fine-tuning the building plans and working with the city for approval. Things were moving along just as we had planned, and our people were so excited about our expansion project.

After a full year of going back and forth with the city, they turned us down and rezoned our property, including some additional land we had purchased, so that it would be nearly impossible to expand. Ever. To say that I was discouraged would be an understatement. No one saw this coming. We had been assured that, while there was some opposition, we would ultimately get the necessary approvals. Our staff and volunteers were looking forward to having more space for ministry. And it was my job to give them the bad news.

I wanted to go to my office, close the blinds, turn off the lights, and turn on some country music. If you are not familiar with that genre of music, the songs are often about something lost, usually love, a dog, or a truck. I felt like we had lost our future. What made it worse was that there was nothing I could do about it.

I'm a preacher, but I'm also a human being. I had preached those verses in Ephesians about how God works everything out according to his plan, and the Romans 8:28 verse that says *all* things work together for good. And then there's that wonderful passage in Jeremiah 29 that says God has plans for us, not to harm us but to give us hope. But when we got that unexpected bad news that we would never be able to expand our facilities, I wasn't feeling much like preaching those verses.

Sometimes I think God takes things out of our control just to show us how much *he's* in control. Sometimes I think he deliberately interrupts our plans so we can see his better plan for us.

After my little self-pity party, we regrouped to figure out what to do next, and that's when we learned we can trust that God is in control, all the time. He used the disappointment of closed doors to stimulate us to think outside of the box. God had a better idea for us, and it took what looked like an unfair zoning law to show it to us. Rather than build a bigger building, what if we just added more services in other locations? We experimented with that idea, which grew into a strategy that is now referred to as "multisite" ministry and is used by churches all over the world. We went from whiners to innovative leaders in the time it took for God to get our attention and remind us he's in control and has a better plan. God knew about the zoning law before we did. Even before the city did. He never has a day when he says, "I never saw that coming." What looked like our biggest disappointment as a church became a source of God's blessing to others. Great planning by a God who is in control even when we're not.

## GOD HAS GUARANTEED A FUTURE FOR YOU

Here's the best part about being loved by a God who is in control: Not only has he chosen you and created a plan for you that will turn your out-of-control moments into experiences of growth and trust, he is in control of your future. As his adopted child, you will share in a great inheritance — living forever in his presence.

I don't know what heaven will be like. The only thing I know is that it will be just right. Perfect. But because the human mind is incapable of truly understanding what heaven will be like, God gives us what I call "God glimpses." Those rare occasions when everything comes together. When you look at a sunset and it is more than beautiful. When you hear a piece of music or see a work of art and it defies description. When you are awed by the majesty of creation, when you see the Creator in the look or actions of a friend or loved one. I believe these are orchestrated by God himself, triggered by the Holy Spirit, to give us a small peek into what heaven, our inheritance, will be like.

And I think he gives those glimpses to us to remind us that something better awaits us. Things won't always go the way you'd like in life. Bad things happen to good people. The world is full of injustice, evil, pain, and disease. While we are here, God wants his family to do their best to make it a better place, but often our best efforts fall short. And sometimes we get discouraged because so many things are beyond our control.

The God who is in control whispers through those images of beauty, "Here's a little taste of what's in your future."

## THE DIVINE SET UP

A good friend of mine used to be the CEO of a major American toy manufacturer. Like anyone who is successful in business, he worked his way up the corporate ladder, honing his leadership skills and developing new ones, as each position required more growth as an executive. He did a great job running the company but decided to take an early retirement so that he could share his skills with a number of nonprofit organizations, including our church. Knowing that there's a big difference between my office and the corner office of the CEO of a major company, I wondered how he was doing, so I asked him if he had any regrets about leaving the corporate world.

"I feel as if my whole career was in preparation for this season of my life," he answered. "It's like God set me up for this."

Of course he has, just as he is using the twists and turns of your life to set you up for something that will bring him glory. When your life seems to be spinning out of control, remember that God chose you and knew about this before he created the world. When you are surprised by one of life's unexpected and unpleasant surprises, remember that God's plan for you will turn your "all things" into something good. And when you are tempted to throw in the towel because your burdens are so heavy and there's nothing you can do, remember that God has a perfect reward waiting for you.

Because he is in complete control.

# CHAPTER 11

# G O D

## IS MERCIFUL

### *Stovall Weems*

Before I was a Christian, I remember having a basic understanding of what Christians believe and what I thought Christianity is all about: basically, that Jesus is the Son of God, that he died for us, and that he rose from the dead. But I didn't understand what that meant for me. Why did I need a Savior, and what was the point of the gospel in my life?

I think many people today face this same type of disconnect. Some may even have a greater difficulty approaching God because of how they view him. When they think of God, they think of a distant superbeing who is not relevant to their lives—or even a harsh God of judgment and wrath. But the very foundation of the gospel is just the opposite. We have a merciful, loving Father who wants to be close to us and be involved in every area of our lives. That's why Jesus came: to rescue us and bring us back to God.

Life as a follower of Christ is not a religion but a relationship. Most of us need to "lose our religion" to gain a real relationship with God through Jesus Christ. That begins by knowing who God is, what he is really like. He is not the harsh, judgmental god who is "out there" somewhere. God loves you as an individual; he cares deeply about you and wants the best for you.

God is merciful.

# PERFECT LOVE

The Bible says we were created for God's glory (Isa. 43:6–7). For many people, the word *glory* can sound kind of mystical. But all it really means is that God created us, that he loves us, and that he designed us to honor him with our lives. We should live our lives in such a way that we reflect God's worth and value to us. He doesn't need us to glorify him because he is on some ego trip. He is not like man in that respect. God is God. He is just fine all by himself. He is the all-sufficient one and does not need anyone or anything to add to his perfection. He is already perfect, awesome, amazing, and omniscient.

God wants us to glorify him because of what it does for us. By experiencing all the wonderful aspects of who he is, we can enjoy a taste of eternity and his eternal attributes right here on this earth and in our everyday lives. He wants to have a relationship with us so he can show us the plan and purpose he has for our lives, one that will give true happiness and satisfaction. When we surrender our lives to Jesus Christ and glorify God, we become happy and fulfilled. It is that simple.

Most people spend their whole lives searching for fulfillment and happiness but never find it. Without God, everyone feels an emptiness they long to fill, not realizing that only God can meet this deepest need. This is why people do crazy, selfish things and end up hurting themselves and each another. They are trying to find happiness in things that cannot satisfy. True happiness is realized only when a person lives for God's glory, not for himself.

Before I came to Jesus, I was all about feeling good. I tried everything possible to make me feel good, but it never lasted. I did all kinds of crazy things, trying to fill the void inside myself, but those paths always led back to emptiness. Before I was willing to surrender my life to Jesus, I had questions about whether God could truly make me happy. I mean, of course I also wanted to go to heaven. I knew that was part of the package deal, and I certainly didn't want to go to hell! But what I really wanted to know was if Jesus could make me feel good. Could I really be fulfilled? Could Jesus make me happy while I was on this earth? Happiness was my quest. And if we dig down deep into our own hearts and are honest with ourselves, we all want happiness. We pursue happiness every day. It's the way God designed us. It's one of our deepest desires, and I wanted to know if God could truly make me happy.

When I looked at Christians, they just seemed boring! Compared with what I was doing, they never seemed like they were having fun. They were never out doing drugs, getting wasted, sleeping around—all of the things I considered normal. So to me it looked like they weren't having any fun, but of course I was just looking at them from the outside. I didn't understand what was going on inside of them. I didn't understand what happens when you begin to *feel* Jesus and *experience* God. When we accept God's mercy and forgiveness, we begin to value God. The reality sets in that we were headed to hell, but now we're headed to heaven. As we feel how much Jesus loves us, we can hardly believe it. We feel joy, peace, even excitement. We begin to walk in the reality of the mercy of God, and it satisfies our souls.

## TRYING TO BE HAPPY

Before I knew Christ, the things I did to make myself happy had to come from the outside. I didn't realize that all those things I was doing could never make me truly happy. But when I received Christ, his Holy Spirit began to change me from the inside out. I suddenly started feeling great because the longing we all feel is actually a longing of the soul that only Jesus can fulfill. I could hardly believe that I was truly happy. That's what the Bible means when it says that he gives you new strength, new peace, and new joy. God gives you good feelings that last, feelings that build you up, feelings that satisfy you. The closer we get to God, the more joy we feel, the more we discover his presence, and the more excited we get about heaven and eternity.

As humans, no matter how much we try in our own strength, we will always fall short of glorifying God the way we should, the way we were made to (Rom. 3:23). That's because deep inside of us is an inclination to do things we know are wrong. The Bible calls it sin. People don't like to talk about sin and sometimes have a hard time believing humans are born with that kind of nature. They want to believe that deep down inside we're all pretty good. And that's the problem. We *are* pretty good, but sin keeps us from being good enough, and that's why we need Jesus. Pretty good isn't enough, and if you look around you and then closely at yourself, you will begin to understand sin. Or to put it another way, if we are all basically good people, why is the world in such bad shape?

Think of sin as not glorifying God as you should. As a result of our sin separating us from God, *all of us* are subject to eternal condemnation. We need forgiveness, and we need to be saved from our sinful and condemned state. We need for the separation thing to be fixed, and we need a new nature that empowers us to live for God and allows us to experience him. The only way that can happen is through Jesus, allowing him into your life as your Savior. When he died on the cross, he actually took your punishment for your sins, so when God looks at you, he sees the innocence of Jesus and pours his mercy over you.

This is the good news of the gospel: Jesus died for you. He paid the price for your sins. By believing this truth for your life, you are no longer separated from God. We call it salvation, and it brings us total forgiveness and gives us a fresh start in life. Eternal life, complete forgiveness, and the innumerable benefits of salvation are given freely to those who repent and put their trust in Jesus Christ.

God doesn't want us to just learn *about* him. That's head knowledge. That's religion. God wants us to *experience* him and have a relationship with him. As Christians, when we begin to trust and believe in Jesus, we receive the Holy Spirit, who comes to dwell on the inside of us. When God gives us his Spirit, we can actually feel him working in our lives. We become who we always wanted to be — free and fully satisfied. Everyone likes to feel good. But true satisfaction that lasts can come only from experiencing God.

Have you ever made a boneheaded, what-in-the-world-was-I-thinking kind of mistake? We've all made mistakes. We've all done things we regret. We've all thought, *I wish I hadn't done that.* You probably can easily think of people you've wronged or people who have hurt you. Life has a way of stacking on the pain. But God's mercy brings us forgiveness that frees us up for a fresh start in him.

Regardless of who you are, what you've done, or where you've been, God wants to pour out his mercy on you. The Bible uses words like *abundant, everlasting,* and *overflowing* to describe his mercy. If a person is convicted of a crime, there's a slight chance he will face a kind judge who will show him a little mercy. Maybe reduce his sentence by a few years. That's not a lot of mercy. It's a little mercy, and the truth is, when it comes to humans, mercy is hard to come by. Not so with God. His mercy is like a huge bucket of water filled to the rim so that if you bumped into it, it would spill all over you. His mercy is so great that he doesn't just forgive us when we fail, but he erases any record of our failure. He doesn't just reduce our sentence — eternal punishment — he eliminates it and sets us free.

## INFINITE MERCY

My favorite description of just how abundant God's mercy is comes in Psalm 103:11: "For as the heavens are high above the earth, so great is His mercy toward those who fear Him" (NKJV). The sun is 93 million miles from the earth. That's millions of miles, but it doesn't stop there. The next closest star to the earth, besides the sun, is 24 billion miles away. So think about it: God compares how high or how far the heavens are above the earth to his mercy. Twenty-four billion miles of mercy is a lot of mercy! Do you know that if you were to travel at the speed of light, it would take you about fifteen days to get there? A light year is the distance you could travel in one year, going 186,000 miles per second. That's almost six trillion miles in a year! Our minds can hardly even comprehend how far that is, yet this is what God chooses to describe the measure of his mercy. Just think: 15,000 miles of distance around the earth, 250,000 miles to the moon, 93 million miles to the sun, and 24 billion miles to the next nearest star. And yet God says as high as the heavens are above the earth, so great is his mercy.

If that's not enough to blow your mind, let's take it even farther. Scientists recently found the farthest galaxy that they can see.

They believe that galaxy is just the beginning of billions and billions more galaxies beyond it. The name of that galaxy is simply a number: A1689-ZD1. It is so high above the earth that it's hard to even explain. If you traveled at the speed of light—remember, that's six trillion miles a year—it would take you 13 billion years to get there, to a galaxy that could be the beginning of billions more! And yet God has even more mercy for you than that.

Maybe you've made mistakes. Maybe you've tried filling that emptiness with other things like I did and you still aren't satisfied. Maybe you've lost hope for the future because try as you might, you can't be the person you want to be. God wants to give you a fresh start. There is no sin or mistake that God's mercy can't cover. You can't use it up. Ever. It is his very nature.

God is merciful.

# CHAPTER 12

# G O D

## IS CLOSE

*Wayne Cordeiro*

*Blessed are those you choose and bring near to live in your courts!
We are filled with the good things of your house, of your holy
temple.*

—Psalm 65:4

When was the last time you saw elephant shapes in the clouds?
Remember when as a kid you would lie on your back in the grass
and see the clouds become animals? We hardly do that anymore,
at least not without guilt. We hardly stop to enjoy a moment just
for the sheer enjoyment of the moment. The day's demands compel
us to make everything urgent. But lately I have been learning that
experiencing God's closeness happens only when I pause to notice
a rainbow or refuse to rush past a sunset. When I take the time to
notice, I feel arising in me a deep sense of his presence that wasn't
there before. I am reminded that I have breath in my lungs, good
friends, and forgiveness, things I've never deserved but have been
granted nonetheless. All because God chose me to be near him.

An old rabbinic saying I heard years ago still haunts me: "One day, God will hold us accountable for all the things he created for us to enjoy, but we refused to do so." God is closest when we are grateful for all those things he has created for us to enjoy.

## STOP SIGNS

Sometimes God sends us a divine directive to be still so he can restore us to himself once again. He removes the hurry from our step in order for us to find him near. I experienced this recently when after several months of chest pains, I learned I had three blockages in my heart. I was put on the next plane from Honolulu to Stanford Medical Center in California. Four days after a successful surgery, I took a detour to our family farm in Oregon to recuperate. There, my two daughters, son-in-law, and two grandchildren live happily alongside thirteen chickens, three dogs, four cats, and one cow. And for a few days, one worn-out pastor.

The timing, as it always is with God, was perfect. My rural recovery began in autumn, one of my favorite seasons, when misty mornings segue into sunny afternoons. I enjoy the chilly, invigorating dawns that eventually surrender to soft rays that creep up and gently warm you. Because of the surgery, I tired easily, but even that was a blessing because I was being ordered to still my soul and simply be grateful I was alive. I slowed my tempo and took in the moment one early October morning as I drove to a nearby coffee shop for devotions. A morning fog lay shrouded on the meadows like cotton. Circling the surrounding hills, a wispy haze created the appearance of a passing train leaving in its wake a trail of steam. Then like a slow, rising curtain, the receding fog revealed a choir of verdant cedars, reminding me of David's great song of praise: "Let the mountains sing together for joy" (Ps. 98:8).

The sun's spotlight introduced the morning scene. The fog danced in ribbons on the surface of a nearby lake and resembled a hundred tiny mystical fairies celebrating the opening act in the dawning sunlight. I was transported back to Camelot, visualizing the Lady in the Lake rising out of a haunting mist. Sunlit dew outlined intricate spider webs adorning the pine trees along our driveway, and smaller webs appeared as snowy ornaments suspended from the upper branches.

The ospreys were in flight that day. They have such a majestic and haunting presence gliding high above the farm. They approached the nearby lake, as their market of choice, to garner an unlucky fish or two for their hatchlings. It was early fall at our family farm, but that morning, it was the opening act of a divine musical that displayed God's splendor all around me. Yet how many times had I driven that same road and missed all that God intended for me to enjoy?

What did you see on your way to work today? As you walked from your car to the front door, did you feel God's breeze brush your face? Did you hear his voice in the chirping of a bird or the rustling of leaves?

## FINDING HIM CLOSE

God's artistry is not limited to the beauty of a rural countryside. It is evident everywhere if we would only stop to notice. We experience gratefulness only when we slow down and notice the banquet God has spread before us.

Listen.

I heard his delight in my granddaughter's laughter. I saw his face in the smile of the waitress who brought me my coffee. I felt his warmth in the sunshine. I sensed his pleasure in the gathering of God's people at our church. I heard him sigh with satisfaction in the rustling of the palm trees near our home, and I was once again so grateful. We must never tire of allowing his artistry to overwhelm us.

God's wake-up call and my subsequent visit to the family farm is but one of many times he has reminded me to slow down and be grateful so I can experience his closeness. I first began learning this from the people of the church I pastor. New Hope, on the Hawaiian island of Oahu, had its humble beginnings thirteen years ago. We haven't been graced with a permanent building yet, so at a high school, one team sets up and another takes down — for five services! At nine other locations, the same scenario is repeated. New Hope requires fifteen hundred volunteers every weekend just so we can have church.

We have become one family in many locations, joined by a common heart for Christ, a love for one another, and a video link. Along with ten other daughter churches, we comprise a constellation of colleagues to reach these beautiful islands with the news of God's love. From the beginning, our people have chosen to be grateful for what we have rather than focus on what we don't have. One acre of Hawaiian real estate is appraised at 2.5 million dollars. We would require a minimum of twenty acres, and even I can do the math on that one: 50 million dollars just for the land, assuming we could find twenty contiguous acres available anywhere near Honolulu. We can either complain about what we do not have, or we can be grateful for what we do. We have chosen the latter, and that is what keeps God close.

Gratefulness differs from thankfulness. Of course, both are essential. Thankfulness is the cordial response to a favor done for you. It is the affirmation you give when things go your way. It is the reply to a gift or a promotion; it's the *hooray* after a blessing. Gratefulness, however, is different and can only be developed intentionally. It begins with a spirit. It's an attitude, a disposition that we carry whether or not things go our way. It's being content *before* any gifts are given. It's breathing a silent "thank you" regardless of what the circumstances are. It's the *hallelujah* with no guarantee of a blessing. It is the confidence to accept gladly whatever God brings.

## EYES THAT SEE

Two people were once walking on the beach as storm clouds approached from the horizon. One complained about how the impending rain would ruin her plans to add to her already deep suntan. The other exclaimed at how majestic the clouds looked and how the rains would bring that fresh smell that she loved just after a storm passes. Both saw the same thing—or did they? How could one see disappointment while the other saw joy?

In Matthew 6:22–23, Jesus said, "The eye is the lamp of the body; so then if your eye is clear, your whole body will be full of light. But if your eye is bad, your whole body will be full of darkness."

Jesus is referring to how we perceive life, to how we choose to see things. It defines the colors on our palette. One person paints things dark, while another paints them bright. One person's tray holds only grays, while another's bounces with neon colors. We choose how we will paint situations, setbacks, and circumstances.

What colors will you choose?

Gratefulness searches for splendor. It takes the time to see the grandeur in the simple. It respects the wisdom that is etched into every line in an elder's countenance. It looks past the pierced lip and searches for the potential within a young and confused street person. Every stroke of the brush has meaning if only we have the eyes to see them with gratefulness.

At our church, we have never tried to attract a specific demographic. I don't even like that word because it dehumanizes what we care most about: people. We just open our doors and whoever comes is welcome. And they come in all ages, shapes, colors, and sizes. We have learned that every person was created by God, and thus, they are all masterpieces. He has given us eyes to see the beauty behind wrinkles, tattoos, bifocals, and beards.

## EARS THAT HEAR

Toward the end of his life, the great composer Beethoven became deaf. The portals that once enchanted his soul were silenced by age. Yet he played. His fingers awakened symphonies only he could imagine. To any normal ear, the music coming from his worn-out piano sounded discordant and dissonant; yet tears would stream down the cheeks of the famed composer as he played. Beethoven was hearing the music the piano *should* make, not what it did make.

Gratefulness is the Beethoven of our churches. It is the ears through which our days may dance again. It hears the sounds of what could be and it guides us with hope. It reminds us of all the gifts that we should not have been given, the friends we do not deserve, and the grace we did not earn.

It is easy to lose this fragile gift. It is readily displaced or unwittingly exchanged for *want*. It slumps into entitlement and tricks us into thinking that we deserve more than we do.

Instead, gratefulness is to be cherished and carefully maintained. It is to be exercised in the shadows as well as in the footlights, equally in the extravagant as in the common. It is more about the condition of our hearts than it is the condition of our houses.

At our church, it would be so easy for people to become discouraged because we don't have a beautiful building. But they have the ears of Beethoven. It's kind of like the way my wife, Anna, and I felt about our first home. Only 780 square feet, it wasn't much; you'll never find it in *Better Homes and Gardens*. But often as we returned from a long day and pulled into the driveway, we would sit for a moment and look at our little home and one of us would say, "What a beautiful home we have." That's what our people feel about our church, even though we don't have a building.

Each weekend, I drive onto the high school campus where New Hope has held weekend services for over a decade. I notice the many tents that have been set up the night before. I see our parking attendants, who arrived at five in the morning, and other volunteers who have helped transform the school's seventy-year-old auditorium, once slated for demolition, into a palace fit for the King. Tears blur my eyes, and I am once again reminded of the treasure we have in our midst. We couldn't do church without them.

All our receptionists at New Hope are volunteers. It's been that way since the beginning. One dear lady has been volunteering every Wednesday for more than four years. Approaching the front desk one day, I stopped to notice her faithfulness and to thank her for taking her only day off to answer phones and greet visitors.

"Oh no!" she replied. "I should thank you!" she said. "I look forward to this all week long. This is where my soul finds rest and my heart is uplifted."

She has the ears of Beethoven. Where others would hear the discordant music of missing their one day off, she hears the symphony of God's closeness.

## LOSING HEART

If we are not intentional, we forget to take the time to notice God's closeness.

Unless we deliberately slow our pace and notice the beauty of God's presence, we quickly fall into our routines and miss what he has in store for us.

In the pioneer days of New Hope, all we had was heart. We didn't have chairs; we sat on cafeteria tables. We didn't have instruments; every musician had to bring his own. But we had heart, and that is all God needed to begin his work with us. We'd set up a gauntlet of greeters, eight on each side, and when people arrived, they were funneled between our grandstands of huggers. We would later be dubbed "the hugging church," known for converging on anyone within ten feet.

We sang with all our hearts. We served with all our hearts. We set up and took down with all our hearts, and the church grew. I remember praying in the early days of New Hope, "God, I pray that one day we will have our *own* chairs, our *own* sound system, and maybe even some paid staff with our *own* office!" I didn't mind working out of my briefcase at a coffee shop, but it wasn't long before our discipleship groups were taking up the dining area. The store manager kindly asked us to find a larger venue, get rid of some people, or buy out the coffee shop.

As the months passed by, we saved enough money to rent our own office space. We bought our own chairs and purchased our own musical instruments. We had our own sound system and even bought our own vans. We had arrived!

One day, however, a lady's innocent comment stopped me in my tracks: "I love the music and I love the drama. We have talented musicians and such wonderful services. I remember the early days when we had little or nothing, but yet we thrived. We had heart. We used to have such big hearts. I am sure it's still there, but it's hard to see anymore. Where's the heart?"

She was right. During this last season, we had flatlined. We began new programs and new initiatives. Checking off all the tasks and measuring the results became more important to us than anything else. Although the heart of New Hope was still present, it was not our top priority. Programs and procedures ruled the day. We were simply *doing* church rather than being the church. This dear lady wasn't complaining; she was just wistful, wondering what had happened. But her comment forced me to my knees that very night as I spent extra time in prayer seeking God's counsel.

I honestly cannot tell you that I heard an audible voice, but I clearly sensed that he was speaking to me, and in so many words, this is what he said: "Correct back to the heart. Peel away whatever you need to until the servant's hearts are once again visible. In the end, a mind will reach a mind, but only a heart will reach a heart."

God directed us to go back to the basics, where people are more important than programs. We placed greater emphasis on "heart issues"—focusing on people and their needs, making sure that worship was from the heart and not a performance, becoming more dependent on God's Holy Spirit than on our own cleverness. That is what God used to grow our church in the beginning, and it is what he would use to grow our church now. We pruned any program or task that relied more on image than heart. We culled initiatives that were based on talent more than on character. We restructured until we could see the light of genuine hearts again.

The apostle Paul's prayer became ours: "I pray that the eyes of your heart may be enlightened, so that you will know ... the riches of the glory of His inheritance in the saints, and what is the surpassing greatness of His power" (Eph. 1:18–19 NASB). We felt God's closeness once again as we became grateful for what really mattered to us as a church.

## DULY REMINDED

Several years ago we held a talent night at our church. We gathered our brightest and best onstage for an evening of concert and drama rich in ambience. From the opening presentation, the full house of enthusiasts knew this would be an evening to remember. Brilliant dances, extraordinary solos, enchanting dramas, and beautiful choreography graced the stage. I sat spellbound realizing how endowed we were as a church.

Toward the end of the evening, the lights dimmed and one of our special children appeared on stage. Nikki has Down syndrome. She and her parents began attending the church when we first started in a junior high school cafeteria. She appeared confident and convinced that she was supposed to be there, except for the fact that she wasn't sure *why*! A few awkward seconds passed, and then Darlene Zschech's beautiful song "Lord, I Give You My Heart" spilled over the sound system. Using American Sign Language, Nikki began.

Her hand motions and demeanor found increasing confidence with each passing lyric, reminding us of the one who gave his life for us. I felt myself drawn to the truth of this reminder, and as I surrendered to it, I felt something deep down being recalibrated. The anthem concluded. With hands upraised, Nikki stood triumphant before us. All activity in heaven seemed stilled for the moment. Tears and sobs overpowered our good manners, and we broke into a standing ovation with shouts of "Encore!"

God gave us that moment, just as he gave me the sunrise over the family farm, to expand our hearts with gratefulness so that we could feel how close he is. All the time. If we would only slow down and be grateful.

# CHAPTER 13

# G O D

## IS NOT

*Steven Furtick*

Every dysfunction begins with a distortion about who God is. That's why, in addition to knowing who he is, it's important to understand who he isn't. Most believers realize that God is holy, sovereign, righteous, pure, majestic, powerful, sufficient, wonderful, and a lot of other adjectives we're pretty familiar with. And we could spend years exploring those attributes and barely scratch the surface. But to set a foundation for our understanding of what God is like, we also have to know what he isn't like. We have to undo those distortions about who he is.

One of the dysfunctions that I see in so many lives—and again and again in my own heart—is the dysfunction of anxiety. Maybe you have no fears. Maybe you're one of those rare people who doesn't worry about your finances because you know God is your source, or about your relationships because you know God is your Father. But most of us get anxious about these kinds of things, and that says a lot about what we truly believe about God.

Anxiety is not only a dysfunction; it's a sin. We may hear more about the sins of lust, greed, bitterness, or anger, but when our hearts are anxious, we reveal a belief that God is not really in control of our lives. When circumstances take a turn for the worse — or even when we think they might — we freak out and act like God took a nap or went on a lunch break. That's an offense toward him — or, in other words, a sin. And that's why we need an accurate understanding of who he is.

The Bible gives us clear instructions: "Do not be anxious about anything, but in everything, by prayer and petition, with thanksgiving, present your requests to God. And the peace of God, which transcends all understanding, will guard your hearts and your minds in Christ Jesus" (Phil. 4:6 – 7). Those words offer a lot of encouragement, but the passage begins with a command: thou shalt not be anxious. The only way we can do that is by knowing who God is — and who he isn't.

Of course, there are many things God is not. He is not angry with us. He is not distant. He is not capricious or unfair. But when it comes to overcoming our anxiety, it would be helpful if we realized that God is not incapable. When we live our lives in a state of panic and anxiety, we infer that God is unable to help us.

## WHEN UNMET NEEDS MEET GOD

Typically, anxiety is a result of an unmet need in our hearts. One of the great characters from the Old Testament knew something about an unmet need and through it came to grips with who God really is. Abraham is the progenitor of our faith. He was an average guy living in Ur (where Iraq is today) when God found him and promised to make a great nation through him. His name was Abram at the time, and things were going well for him except that he had no heir to carry on his legacy. God had already given him great wealth and helped him win many victories over his enemies. Still, Abram couldn't have a child, and without a child, he had no heir. According to the custom of the day, if you didn't have a son, the main servant of the household would receive the inheritance and carry on the family's legacy. That didn't seem to fit the promise of someone who would one day be a father of nations. Abram needed a son, and it didn't look like that would ever happen. Knowing how something like this could cause him to worry, God appeared to Abram and encouraged him: "Do not be afraid, Abram. I am your shield, your very great reward" (Gen. 15:1). That should have been a comforting thing to hear from the God who made heaven and earth. "I am your defense and your offense," God was essentially saying. "I'm going to protect you and provide for you. It's already taken care of, so just go about your business and trust me."

Abram wasn't so sure: "O Sovereign LORD, what can you give me since I remain childless and the one who will inherit my estate is Eliezer of Damascus? . . . You have given me no children; so a servant in my household will be my heir" (vv. 2 – 3).

Just as we do so many times, Abram felt it necessary to explain his situation to God. As if God didn't already know. He was anxious because he did not trust God. In this short response, he demonstrates his view of God as incapable of fulfilling his own promise. What can the God who *made* him give to him? The question is almost an accusation that God is untrustworthy, that there are some things he just can't do. How do you call God sovereign and then start by questioning what he can do? We do it all the time. At least Abram had some reason to be incredulous. He and his wife were old and wrinkled, yet God was talking about giving him a son. Look at the kinds of things that make us anxious:

- Am I going to be able to pay all my bills this month?
- Will I get that promotion?
- I sure hope it doesn't rain during our vacation.
- Can we afford to send her to private school?

We get anxious even about things that are logically possible, so we can't really point fingers at Abram. He had been promised something that was logically impossible. But God is the God of impossibilities. Creating the universe from nothing was pretty big — the rest is child's play for God. Yet we pray with such little faith and little expectation because we just aren't sure he can get the job done.

Once when I was trying to illustrate the way we Christians let anxiety weigh us down, I asked a kid to come up on the platform and get on my back, and for the next few minutes as I preached, I carried him around until he got so heavy I had to lower him back to the platform. I wanted our people to have a visual reminder of what anxiety looks like—a burden that we don't really need to carry. I *chose* to carry that child on my back. I didn't have to. He was perfectly content to stay in his seat (well, at least as content as any kid could be listening to a sermon). For the few minutes he was on my back, the weight impeded my ability to walk freely.

God invites us to get rid of that burden of worry and reassures us that he's strong enough to carry it for us. "Cast all your anxiety on him because he cares for you" (1 Peter 5:7). His care is complete and thorough.

## THE SPIRITUAL STUFF

None of us, of course, would actually admit that we think God is incapable, that there are some things he just can't do. We have learned all the right words to describe his competence: he's got the whole world in his hands; he's always in control; he's on the throne; he can do anything; he alone is the sovereign God. So the issue isn't necessarily that we believe God is incapable. The real issue is that we believe certain areas of our lives are outside the realm of his expertise. He's good at the spiritual stuff, but when it comes to our practical needs—or even our more personal ones—well, we aren't so sure.

Even after believing God and having his faith credited to him as righteousness (Gen. 15:6), Abram seemed to wonder if God still needed some help. He got tired of waiting for the promised son to come. He had seen God move in plenty of other areas of his life, but he had trouble believing and waiting for the promised son. Maybe childbearing just wasn't God's specialty after all. So when Abram's wife suggested that he sleep with her maid, Hagar, he said, "Yes, dear." The son that resulted from that union caused nothing but pain and trouble. Whenever we try to help God out—whenever we go outside his boundaries to get what we need—it brings nothing but chaos, controversy, and conflict to our lives. When we assume there's an area of our lives outside the realm of God's expertise, we invite disaster.

I once was having a conversation with a businessman who was being tempted to compromise his integrity to make a dollar. I think he wanted me to sort of bless his intention to cut some ethical corners, but I couldn't. I told him I thought he should do what was honest and right and that God would honor him for that. Like a lot of people in the business world, he thought a preacher like me couldn't understand how things are in the real world. "Preacher," he said, "that might work in the ministry, but this is business we're talking about."

Really? Integrity might work in the ministry, but there's a different set of rules for other areas of life? That would mean that even though God is competent with spiritual things like saving souls, we're on our own when we go to work; we have to work things out for ourselves in the "secular" world, or to "sleep with Hagar" to get what we really need. But God doesn't work like that. He can create a profit in our businesses on his own terms, even if his terms don't make "good business sense." He can handle relationships and children and much, much more. He's capable in every area of life. He even knows where to fish.

Do you remember the story from the gospel of Luke about the time the disciples had been fishing all night yet had caught nothing? With more than a hint of sarcasm, Jesus came up to them and said, "Hey guys, have you caught anything?" He knew they hadn't, but I think he was just having some fun with his omniscience. When they acknowledged what he already knew, he told them to move to another location and try again. Peter was a professional fisherman and may have wondered if Jesus really understood how things work in the real world. This was a commercial fishing boat. These guys weren't fishing just for the fun of it. This was their livelihood, and they had been doing it all their lives. So when this religious guy shows up and tells them where to fish, they probably rolled their eyes at each other and maybe even thought of just ignoring him. But Peter complied, and the Bible says they caught so many fish that the nets started breaking and they couldn't figure out how to get them all in the boat. Peter could have said, "You do the religious teaching and leave the fishing to us. You focus on the church thing, and we'll do business in the real world." That's how a lot of us approach God. But Peter, in spite of his reluctance, knew Jesus was Lord over every area of life. And Jesus showed him clearly how capable God is.

I've known a lot of people who are pretty good at trusting God for spiritual things but can't trust him for relationships. When it comes to whom you should date or decisions you make about marriage, a lot of people think you have to "sleep with Hagar" because God's only the soul doctor, not the love doctor. But God was the first matchmaker. He set Adam up on a blind date — really blind, since he put Adam to sleep while he made Eve — and the results were wildly successful. God still has the ability to orchestrate the affairs of every area of your life.

What a lot of us haven't comprehended is that God cares about every area of our lives and is capable of meeting our physical needs just as easily as he meets our spiritual needs. There's no area outside the realm of his expertise, and there's no distinction between "spiritual" and everything else. You don't have a spiritual life; you *are* a spiritual life. You are a spirit living in a body, both of which God created, and everything he says to you is helpful for your instruction. If he isn't capable of seeing you through your relationships or of providing for you in your finances, if he's not worthy of your trust in every area of your life, no matter how insignificant, how can you trust him with your eternity and the salvation of your soul? If God is capable with the biggest issues of life, he's capable with all of them.

## NOTHING'S TOO BIG

My son Elijah came to me a few weeks ago when I was working out — or "extra-sizing," as he calls it — and told me he wanted his pirate ship brought downstairs for him. It's huge, much too big for him to carry, and he was begging me to get it for him. But I was too busy and kept telling him I couldn't do it then. Finally, he said, "Daddy, I really need my pirate ship. Do you think you're strong enough to do that for me?" Now that's a smart kid; he knew how to appeal to my pride, the one motivating factor that could get me to respond to him. But his question reminds me of the way a lot of us approach God when we have a big problem on our hands. We know it's too big for us, but we also act as if it's too big for God. Why worry and try to do all the heavy lifting by yourself when you have this kind of God on your side:

"For the LORD your God is God of gods and Lord of lords, the
great God, mighty and awesome" (Deut. 10:17).

"Who is this King of glory? The LORD strong and mighty, the
LORD mighty in battle" (Ps. 24:8).

"Yet their Redeemer is strong; the LORD Almighty is his name"
(Jer. 50:34).

"The God we serve is able to save us" (Dan. 3:17).

"The arm of the LORD is not too short to save, nor his ear too
dull to hear" (Isa. 59:1).

When we align our view of God with the way he is described in
the Bible, we realize that there is nothing God cannot do.

Abram eventually got what he wanted, but his lack of trust
caused him great anxiety, just as it does for all of us. I sometimes
wonder why some people bother to pray if they don't really think
God is capable or interested in answering them. Eventually, Abram
came to understand that God is trustworthy, and that gave him
the confidence he needed to become one of the great patriarchs of
our faith. God didn't beat Abram down for his doubts. He assured
Abram that a son from his own body would be born and become his
heir. He raised Abram's vision: "Look up at the heavens and count
the stars — if indeed you can count them.... So shall your offspring
be" (Gen. 15:5). And Abram believed God, and it was credited to
him as righteousness.

As I write this, our nation is in the midst of tremendous eco-
nomic upheaval. Millions of breadwinners are out of work. People
who have lived in their homes for twenty years and more are facing
foreclosure. Our sons and daughters are fighting wars in Afghani-
stan and Iraq, and the rise of terrorism threatens at home and
abroad. I know these are all complex issues, but I often wonder
what would happen if we truly believed God is capable of fixing
banks and businesses. What would our world look like if Christians
everywhere would unite behind this benediction that the apostle
Paul gave to the church at Ephesus: "God is able to do immeasurably
more than all we ask."

# CHAPTER 14

# GOD
## IS BIG

*Gary Shiohama*

When I was a kid, I believed in Buddha. My parents set up a small Buddhist altar in our home, and as a youngster, I would dutifully bow and offer incense to the image of Buddha in the altar. Since I paid homage to Buddha as I was taught, I assumed that he was God. It wasn't until years later that I learned that Buddha never claimed to be deity, he never displayed any miraculous powers, and he died around 483 B.C. Buddha wasn't God. He was just an ordinary human being.

Yet millions of people have idolized and deified him under the mistaken assumption that he's a god. But he's not any more of a god than you or I. The psalmist said that "the idols of the nations are silver and gold, made by the hands of men. They have mouths, but cannot speak, eyes, but they cannot see; they have ears, but cannot hear, nor is there breath in their mouths" (Ps. 135:15 – 17). If a man can make a god, it would have to be pretty puny. I've seen pictures of some of the largest Buddhas in the world, and while they're pretty big, they're actually tiny when it comes to the one true God. Because God is big. Really big!

# BIG FINGERS

One of the things I like to do with my youngest daughter, Natalie, is thumb wrestle. I enjoy it because it's fun, it's cheap, and I always win. I also enjoy it when someone with strong thumbs and fingers massages my back. There are other things you can do with your fingers, like paint your nails, as my oldest daughter likes to do. You can also use your finger to point at someone and yell, "Hey you, wake up!" That's something I'm tempted to do every time I speak at church. A lot of folks like to lick their fingers after eating a good meal. KFC claims its chicken is "finger lickin' good."

Here's what God likes to do with his fingers: run them across the earth out west to form the Grand Canyon. Or pinch some dirt together to form Mount Everest. It's true! Here's what the Bible says: "When I consider your heavens, the work of your fingers, the moon and the stars, which you have set in place, what is man that you are mindful of him, the son of man that you care for him?" (Ps. 8:3–4).

God is so big that all he needed to create the universe were his fingers.

Actually, he didn't literally use his fingers to create stuff. David wrote that about God's fingers because he knew that humans cannot really comprehend how big God is, and so he used human characteristics to describe him. It's a literary technique called *anthropomorphism*, something poets used to help us wrap our human minds around the divine. In another psalm, David said that God spoke the universe into existence. I really don't know how the earth was formed; even the smartest scientists who study these things don't know for sure. What I do know for sure is that it took a really big God to give us the universe.

Consider just this one planet we call home. Scientists estimate the weight of the earth to be six sextillion tons. If you're wondering how much six sextillion is, it's a six followed by twenty-one zeroes. By any stretch of the imagination, six sextillion tons is heavy. Yet as heavy as the earth is, it's not plummeting uncontrollably through space. All six sextillion tons is suspended in nothingness, held in place by an unseen force scientists call gravity; but in reality it's held in place by our big God. According to the Scriptures, "He spreads out the northern skies over empty space; he suspends the earth over nothing" (Job 26:7).

And not only does he suspend the earth over nothing, God tilted the earth at a twenty-three degree angle so we can experience winter, spring, summer, and fall. He also spins the earth on an invisible axis at the rate of one thousand miles an hour so we can have night and day. Then he orbits this six sextillion ton behemoth we call home around the sun at the rate of sixty-seven thousand miles an hour. At that speed it's a wonder none of us have been blown off the earth! And how does he do it? He must be really big.

One year when I was at Hume Lake, which is located in Sequoia National Park, I had the opportunity to observe Jupiter through a telescope. Jupiter is the largest planet in our solar system, and it's more than 390 million miles away. Yet I was able to distinctly make out four of its sixty-three moons, which God placed there with the snap of his fingers (anthropomorphically speaking). Jupiter and the earth are just two planets in a universe of billions of galaxies that God created, and that he suspends in nothingness.

Brennan Manning wrote in his book *The Ragamuffin Gospel* that if you held out a dime at arm's length while gazing at the night sky, the coin would block out 15 million stars from your view, if your eyes had the power to see that far into space. Manning's observation reminds me of what God said to Abraham: "Look up at the heavens and count the stars—if indeed you can count them" (Gen. 15:5). After looking up, Abraham surely must have concluded that God is big, and that he has big fingers.

## TINY HUMANS

A few years ago I was doing some yard work when I heard a faint meow. So I poked around the bushes with my rake and discovered a tiny kitten, probably not more than a couple of weeks old. I didn't tell my wife or kids (I've got two girls), because I knew that they would want to keep it. And there's no way I wanted a cat, because I hate cats. So I left the kitty alone, but checked on it periodically throughout the day.

By the time evening rolled around, the kitty's meows sounded more desperate and pleading. From what I could determine, the mother had abandoned her helpless kitty. Compassion got the best of me; I told my wife and kids, and they quickly scrambled to the kitty's aid. Meanwhile I was dispatched on a mercy of mission to the pet store to buy some milk. About an hour later, I returned home with an expensive kitty formula. (Apparently kittens shouldn't drink cow's milk, and I'm not good at milking cats.) After the famished kitten ate, my daughters asked, "What are we going to name it?" Name it? Why would we name it if we're not going to keep it? Too late. On that day, "Megan" joined our family.

We soon discovered two startling facts: Megan was a he, and he had hundreds of friends. He was infested with fleas, and since he was too young to be treated with flea spray, we had to pick those disgusting critters off him by hand. Did you know that a flea is only one-sixteenth to one-eighth of an inch long and can jump two hundred times its own body length? They are so tiny and my fingers are so big.

That must be how God feels when he deals with us. Compared with him, we are so tiny. If his fingers can figuratively put the planets in place, how small must we seem to him. And yet he cares for us individually, day and night. He listens to us when we cry out to him. He provides for us, knowing what we need even before we ask.

King David, overwhelmed with God's ability to take care of us, asked rhetorically, "What is man that you are mindful of him, the son of man that you care for him?" (Ps. 8:3–4). In other words, isn't it amazing that a God so big can care for every tiny human? We must seem like fleas to him, yet he reaches down and lifts us up when we fall and even shares some of his strength with us so that we can make it through difficult times.

Aren't you glad God is so big?

# BLIMP-SIZED PRAYERS

A few years ago, a boy who attended our junior high school group wanted to ride on the Goodyear blimp. The *Spirit of America* was parked right off the 405 Freeway not far from our church, and every Sunday on his way to church, it would catch Eric's eye. So one day he asked his mom, Pat, who is a schoolteacher, if he could ride the Goodyear blimp. His mom told him, "No, Eric, you can't ride the Goodyear blimp. It's not like a ride at Disneyland. You have to know someone to ride the blimp, and we don't know anyone. So you might as well forget it, Eric, because you're never going to ride it."

Eric's mom effectively slammed the door shut on her son's dream, but Eric was not dissuaded. He told his mom, "I'm going to pray about it."

About a week later, one of Pat's students had to leave class early for what she assumed was a doctor's appointment. When the mom showed up to take her son out of class, Pat asked why he had to leave. The mom replied, "Today's a special day because Tristan is going for a ride on the Goodyear blimp." As you can imagine, Pat's jaw hit the floor! It turned out that Tristan's grandfather knew someone at Goodyear who arranged for people to ride the blimp. When the boy's mother saw Pat's jaw drop, she asked if something was wrong. So Pat told her about Eric's prayer, and ten days later, Eric and his mom were soaring through the skies of Southern California on the Goodyear blimp. Coincidence you say? No way! Eric and his mom got the ride of their lives because of his childlike faith in a great big God.

In his prayer for the church at Ephesus, the apostle Paul described what Eric knew all along: "Now to him who is able *to do immeasurably more* than all we ask or imagine, according to his power that is at work within us, to him be glory in the church and in Christ Jesus throughout all generations, for ever and ever! Amen" (Eph. 3:20–21, emphasis added). Paul said that God is so big, he is able to do *way* more than we ask him to do. Not only that, God is so big, he is able to do way more than we *imagine* he can do. Do you believe that? Eric did. The difference between a blimp rider and the rest of us who will only see the *Spirit of America* in the skies above us is childlike faith in a big God with unlimited power.

Do you believe that God is *that* big?

## THE BIG GOD WHO BECAME SMALL

When Joey Everett, our worship leader, was eighteen years old, he learned he had cancer. Shortly before Christmas, Joey was admitted to the hospital to undergo a twelve-hour lymphectomy because the cancer had spread to his lymph nodes. He was told that the procedure would require multiple blood transfusions and an incision that would extend from his chest to his pelvis. Joey was terrified.

Before going to the hospital that morning, Joey opened up his Bible and read, "When I consider your heavens, the work of your fingers, the moon and the stars, which you have set in place, what is man that you are mindful of him, the son of man that you care for him?" (Ps. 8:3–4). Joey said the verse reminded him that God is big, but as he put it, "I was still scared!"

A few hours later, Joey found himself all alone lying on a gurney in the surgery prep room. He was just minutes away from being rolled into the operating room, and with tears rolling down his cheeks, Joey prayed, "God, I know you're big. Please be with me, and let me feel your presence." Even before he could sign off with an "amen," Joey said that out of nowhere, the lovely carol "Silent Night" started to play on the hospital loudspeaker above him.

He said it was the most beautiful sound he had ever heard. Even though he had listened to the song hundreds of times before, he felt this time it was as if God played it just to remind him that a very big God became small for his sake. God is big, but he made himself small enough to be born in a manger, small enough to fit on a cross, small enough to live in our hearts. And on that December day, small enough to be in the hospital room with Joey.

I'm glad God is big enough to make himself small. I'm glad that he found a way to enter our lives through his Son, Jesus. My disappointment at learning that Buddha wasn't a god gave way to rejoicing when I met the one true God who set the world in place with his little finger.

Whatever you are up against, God is bigger.

# CHAPTER 15

# G O D

# IS NOT LIKE ME

*Toby Slough*

From the instant God made man in his own image, as recorded in Genesis 1:27, we've been trying to reverse the process. We want him to be just like us — to act and think like us — and when he doesn't, it frustrates us. There have been times when I've wanted God to smack down someone who was mean to me, because that's what I would do. I've never prayed for him to do that, but secretly I expected him to do some payback for me. So far, he's never done it, and it just drives me crazy when God doesn't act more like me.

Some people get a little nervous when I say things like, "God drives me crazy," but I learned at an early age that God can take our frustrations with him. I was the kid who gave my Sunday school teacher gray hair because I always seemed to ask the taboo questions, the questions everyone *wanted* to ask but were afraid to. Not me. My poor teacher would teach us things like you should turn the other cheek or it is hard for rich people to go to heaven, and I'd ask why. I wasn't trying to be obstinate or a smart aleck; I really wanted to know, and I was never satisfied with the typical Sunday-school answer.

Thankfully, my teacher was a wise woman — or maybe I just wore her out with my questions — but after three or four why's in a row, she always referred me to this verse from the Old Testament: "The Lord says, 'My thoughts are not like your thoughts. Your ways are not like my ways. Just as the heavens are higher than the earth, so are my ways higher than your ways and my thoughts higher than your thoughts' " (Isa. 55:8–9 NCV).

I have to give her credit. Because she didn't try to shut me up or get angry with me for asking so many questions, to this day I am confident that our faith can stand up to any questioning. But she also taught me something else by continually referring me to that verse: God does things his own way, and his way is right no matter what. I'm glad God isn't like me, because I'm *not* always right. In fact, I'm wrong a lot. As I've grown in my faith, this verse has given me great comfort, even when I can't predict what God will do next. I want to serve a God who is bigger than me, one whom I can't fully comprehend or understand. I don't want a god you can put in a box. I don't want a god that runs with programs and formulas. Even now, when I wonder why God didn't answer a prayer the way I wanted him to or allowed something to happen to me that I can't understand, I can almost hear him whispering, "My ways are not your ways. My thoughts are not your thoughts."

I'm *glad* God is not like me.

## GOD'S SCHEDULE IS DIFFERENT FROM MINE

The clock tick-tocks loudly. The strong smell of medication and clean, crisp sheets permeates the small room. By now, you've worn out the carpet with pacing. You've read every magazine twice. You've even attempted to count the number of holes in the drop ceiling. But nothing can keep your mind off of the fact that it's been six hours and still you've heard nothing from the doctor. Nurses have changed shifts, patients have come and gone, and you?

You're still waiting.

I don't know about you, but I don't wait very well. I'm one of those guys who jinxes the checkout line at the grocery store. It was moving smoothly and then after I got in line, the register malfunctioned or the clerk had to call for a price check. Three times. While steam rises from my forehead. When I have to wait, I find stuff bubbling up in me that I didn't even know was there. If I get stuck behind a person driving below the speed limit, anger just wells up in me, and I have no idea where it comes from.

Waiting is infuriating and frustrating; patience is not wired into our DNA. And yet God specializes in making people wait. If we are patient and pay attention, we discover that he shows up in these "waiting rooms of life."

Many of the great stories we treasure from the Bible involve waiting. Abraham and Sarah waited until well past their fertile years to have a child. The Israelites had to wait for forty years before God let them enter the land he had promised them. Do you realize that during the time between the end of the Old Testament and the beginning of the New Testament, there were thousands of God-fearing people who were waiting for the promised Messiah? That one page-flip from Zechariah to Matthew took nearly four hundred years! You'd think under the new covenant, God would move a little faster, but the Bible tells us that the command of God to those disciples gathered in the book of Acts was "to wait" and Jesus would appear to them.

God's schedule is so much different from our frantic rush through life. From Genesis to Revelation, the clear call from God is to wait, but I don't think God just wants to frustrate us. He always has our best interests in mind, and we begin to understand the waiting game when we read this well-known promise from the prophet Isaiah: "But those who wait on the LORD shall renew their strength; they shall mount up with wings like eagles" (Isaiah 40:31 NKJV). In the Hebrew, *wait* has the meaning of "eager anticipation." God wants you to wait with the hope that something is about to happen. Eugene Peterson used the word *trust* instead of wait in his paraphrase, *The Message*, and that really captures what waiting is all about to the Christian. Things start to change in our hearts when we trust in the Lord during times of waiting, delay, and tarrying.

Our schedule is all about instant gratification. We pretty much get what we want, when we want it. If I want to watch the news, I don't have to wait until six o'clock. I can flip on CNN or go to any number of online news sources and see the news instantly. If I want an orange, I don't have to wait until the citrus trees begin bearing fruit in California. I can walk into any grocery store any time of the year and buy an orange. And I can even avoid the risk of getting in the wrong checkout line by speeding through the self-serve line.

It is in this fast-paced environment that God comes to us on a schedule different from ours. When we ask God for things, sometimes he says yes. Sometimes he says no. Most of the time he says, "Not yet." No wonder we get frustrated; we're so used to placing our order at the drive-thru window and then picking it up in a minute or two. Why can't God offer a drive-thru?

Of course, he can. When he wanted light, he spoke it into existence. Immediately. Jesus healed the blind man in the time it took to rub some mud on his face, and when you confessed your belief in him, you were given the gift of eternal life. Immediately. It's not that God is unable to do things quickly. He just sometimes chooses to take his time, and when he does, it is always for our benefit. We want everything now, but God wants what's best and is willing to make us wait so that we get what *he* wants for us.

Remember this as you wait: God isn't doing something *to* you but something *in* you. From the moment you were conceived, the Bible says, God has been working overtime for one reason and one reason only: he wants to draw you to himself. From the moment you gave your heart to Christ, the Spirit of God invaded your soul. God has one goal in mind: for your character and nature to reflect the heart of God. He wants your heart to break for the things that break his heart, that your character, your nature, your decision-making process, your perspective in the world would be lined up with *his* character and nature. God is ready and willing to use anything at his disposal to transform you and refine you into his nature and character. A lot of times that means putting you on a different schedule—his schedule.

Can you imagine being in a hospital waiting room while a team of surgeons is performing delicate surgery on a loved one? Waiting to hear how the surgery went would be extremely difficult, but would you ever think of asking a nurse to go into the operating room to tell the surgeons to hurry up? Of course not, because we want to give them all the time they need to do the best job possible. We believe that they know what they're doing, and if it takes a little longer to make sure our loved one recovers, we're all for it.

God is on a schedule different from the one we are on. When he doesn't come through for us the moment we ask him for something, it doesn't mean he doesn't care or that he has abandoned us. He knows exactly what he is doing. In my own life, it's during that agonizing wait for God's answer that I have grown the most. As Peter reminds us, the wait may be more important than the final answer from God: "Friends, when life gets really difficult, don't jump to the conclusion that God isn't on the job. Instead, be glad that you are in the very thick of what Christ experienced. This is a spiritual refining process, with glory just around the corner" (1 Peter 4:12–13 MSG).

I have come to be thankful that God is not like me. I'm glad he cares enough about me to slow me down and make me wait. His schedule is just right; he's never early and he's never late. "You see, at just the right time, when we were still powerless, Christ died for the ungodly" (Rom. 5:6).

Perfect timing.

## GOD SEES THINGS DIFFERENTLY

If one of your children were sick and you called the doctor's office for help and only got an answering machine, you'd be a little upset, but you'd leave a message and wait for the doctor to call back. If it took the office two days to get back to you, you'd be justified in wanting to switch doctors. That's sort of what happened when Martha and Mary sent word to Jesus that their brother, Lazarus, was sick. Jesus got the news, and despite the fact that he was very close to Lazarus, the Bible says "he stayed where he was two more days." By the time Jesus showed up, Lazarus had died.

Talk about disappointment: " 'Lord,' Martha said to Jesus, 'if you had been here, my brother would not have died' " (John 11:21). She was a lot more polite about it than I might have been: "What were you thinking? I called you two days ago, and you just now show up. Thanks a lot, Jesus, but he's dead!"

Except Jesus didn't quite see it that way. God sees things differently than we do. Where we see problems and disappointments, God sees opportunities. When we go to him with a problem, expecting him to solve it, he tells us to take another look. What we see as bad, he sees as good because he knows what it will do for you: make us more like his Son, Jesus.

One of the reasons I'm not a big fan of those Christian self-help books that promise solutions to our problems if we just follow their seven steps is that it leads us to believe that the Christian life should be trouble-free. I don't think the authors of those books intend to mislead us, and I know people have been helped by those books, but I can't tell you how many people who have come to me complaining, "Toby, I did all the steps and it didn't work." I have to tell them that being a Christian doesn't mean we will never have any problems and that God never promised to make problems disappear. Instead, God sees our problems as an opportunity to help us rely on him more for strength and to grow in spiritual maturity.

Here's one of those ironies that's pretty typical for Christians: when things are going well in our lives, we are often distant from God, but when we are overwhelmed with problems, God is closer. I know that in my own life, when I'm nervous about our family's finances and my wife and I are struggling in our relationship, and the pressures of being a pastor close in on me, and my heart races with worry, I'm forced to cry out to God and he is always right there. But when I've resolved all those problems and get back on track, I tend to go on autopilot and drift a little, and God doesn't feel as close. I'm more likely to tune in to ESPN radio daily than turn to God. Nothing needs to be fixed, so why bother God? We fall into this trap because we don't see things the way God does.

Not only does God see problems as opportunities to help us grow and mature, he sees them as ways to build our endurance. When it comes to the race set before us as believers, God wants long-distance runners, not sprinters.

One day I decided to get in shape. I told my wife I was heading out to the high school track, and she gave me one of those looks. You know, the look that says, "Have you lost your mind?" I reassured her that I was only going to run a couple of miles and then come back home. I drove over to the track, arriving just as a PE class ambled out onto the field, and it was clear they were curious to see what "the old guy" was up to. I'm afraid I disappointed them, for about halfway around the first lap, I was convinced I was about to meet Jesus! Seriously. My heart raced, my chest tightened, and my legs felt like rubber bands. I faked a pulled hamstring, and limped off the track toward my car. I tried to sneak in without Mika noticing, but she caught me. "How'd it go?" she asked. "Fine," I lied. Then I snuck off to call a friend of mine who has been running for years, hoping he could give me some tips.

"I need help, man. I'm thirty-seven years old and I can't run half a lap," I complained.

He gave me the best advice I've ever had, when it relates to any kind of exercise. "Tomorrow, go out and try to run just ten yards past where you ran today." So I did, and then each day after that, I tried to go just a little bit farther until I was adding one more minute, then three more minutes, then one more mile until I had built up enough endurance to run long distances without having to stop for a rest. I became the runner that I never thought I could become.

God sees our problems as ways to help us become the followers we thought we would never become. Instead of trying to "get in shape" in a day, like I did, we can, with God's help, go a little farther each day and allow our problems to shape us into stronger Christians: "Dear brothers and sisters, when troubles come your way, consider it an opportunity for great joy. For you know that when your faith is tested, your endurance has a chance to grow. So let it grow, for when your endurance is fully developed, you will be perfect and complete, needing nothing" (James 1:2–4 NLT).

When we're in the middle of our troubles, we don't always feel like taking that extra step to build our endurance. I'll admit that going just that extra ten yards that second day of my quick plan to get in shape seemed like going another ten miles, and I didn't think I could make it. But now I look back on it and realize it was worth it. I'm much better off now because I pushed through the pain day after day until it finally paid off, and I'm glad I looked at my initial failure through the eyes of an expert.

God knows what you're going through and will give you the strength to go another ten yards and then another ten minutes and then another mile until you break through into a better place. You will look back, as I did, and be amazed that you made it. But you will also be better prepared for the next problem that comes your way, because it will. Problems always do: "In this world you will have trouble. But take heart! I have overcome the world" (John 16:33).

## GOD LOVES DIFFERENTLY

I'm glad God is different than I am when it comes to his time schedule. I'm also glad that he sees things differently than I do, and I am continually trying to adjust my vision so that I can see the way he does. But I am mostly glad that God loves differently than I do. As a human, I'm painfully aware that my love for others is imperfect. As much as I love my wife, I'll be the first to admit that I don't always show it. Don't get me wrong. I love her dearly and would do anything for her, even if it means sacrificing my life for her. But I know there have been times when I've let things come between us that tested her patience and put pressure on our relationship. I know that I've let her down and disappointed her, and I am always grateful when she forgives me. I just wish I could be more consistent and make her feel how loved she is all the time, but I'm human.

It's sobering to consider the fact that roughly half of all marriages end in divorce, because at one point, each of those unsuccessful marriages involved two people very much in love who pledged that they would never, ever stop loving each other.

When it comes to love, aren't you glad God loves differently than we humans do? God's love is perfect. Flawless. He never stops loving us no matter what we do. He loves me the way I wish I could love others.

As a teenager, I really pushed the limits with my mom. My dad was a coach, school administrator, and basketball referee then and traveled all over the place, so for a lot of those years, it was just my mom and me. If a line could be pushed, I pushed it, and I'll never forget one time when I went way over that line. She knew it, I knew it, and to be honest I knew I deserved whatever punishment she had in store for me. But instead of being angry, she grabbed me by the shoulders, looked straight into my eyes, and with tears streaming down her cheeks said, "There's *nothing* you can do to ever make me stop loving you."

That's how God loves us. Essentially he tells us, "There are no deal breakers with me." I meet and talk with people on a weekly basis who struggle with issues in their lives, and the cause is that they truly believe they have done things that have made them unlovable to God. It is inconceivable to them that God loves them regardless of what they have done, because they have experienced only imperfect, human love. They know how quickly a "loved one" has turned on them. They know how easily they have turned their backs on people they love. And they think that must be how God loves too. But he doesn't. The Bible promises us that God "will not abandon you or destroy you or forget the solemn covenant he made with your ancestors" (Deut. 4:31 NLT). Where our love is fickle and often temporary, "his love endures forever" (Ps. 100:5).

I'm still pretty impatient, but I'm working on it. When God says "wait," I remind myself that he has my best interests in mind. I have my share of problems, but I'm trying to see them the way God sees them because I know I need endurance to finish the race. And when it comes to love, I'm just thankful I have a wife who loves me even when I'm not always the most lovable guy in the world.

God is not like me, and he's not like you either. And for that, we can be thankful.

# CHAPTER 16

# G O D

## IS MORE

*Chris Hodges*

In early 2008, several buddies and I went to Florida to celebrate another friend's birthday. One evening after dinner, the eight of us decided to go see the movie *The Bucket List*. I'm not much of a moviegoer, so my expectations weren't very high. But to my surprise, God used the movie as a turning point in my life.

*The Bucket List* is the story of two men from different backgrounds who met as patients in a cancer ward. They eventually became friends and together made a list of things that they wanted to do before they "kicked the bucket."

If you've seen the movie, you know that there is a wonderful moral to the story: that all the thrills in the world can't satisfy the soul like a few eternal things. Things like relationships, laughter, and living your life in a way that makes a difference.

The movie inspired me. At forty-four years old, I was already settling in and had started coasting through life. I realized I was at my halfway point in life and was no longer dreaming of the future. Instead, I was maintaining the status quo: five kids, a good marriage, and a good church. There's nothing really wrong with that, but I left Florida and returned home with a goal to make my own bucket list. Maybe you have your own list.

In my first draft, I wrote down twenty-five big dreams, things like:

1. Celebrate an anniversary in Italy.
2. Take a pilgrimage to the Holy Land.
3. Fly in an F-16 jet.
4. Play Augusta National Golf Club.
5. Write a book (that people actually read).
6. Build my dream home.
7. Make enough money so I can reverse tithe—give ninety percent annually and live on ten percent.
8. Go to every Major League baseball park with one of my four boys.

I was amazed how this fun little exercise stirred in me a passion to live a richer, fuller life. I realized that complacency in any area of my life would lead to a life void of purpose and meaning.

The same is true spiritually: if we stop growing and settle into maintenance and survival mode, we will eventually waste away. That sounds harsh, but I'm convinced it's true.

During my twenty-six years of ministry, I've seen so many Christians just coasting through life. They've got their fire insurance and feel they have eternity locked down, so they're content to leave it at that.

I've seen people who have been in church for a long time, so long that at any given moment of a service they can predict what will happen next. When the speaker makes a point, they're turning to the Scripture reference before he even names it. It becomes almost a game for them; you can see them thinking smugly, *Oh yeah, I know that one. Been there, heard that.*

Some have gone through the routine for so long that their faith has become stale. That's a dangerous place to be. The enemy capitalizes on that complacency to keep us content with where we are, never reaching the potential God has for us.

Watching *The Bucket List* made me want more out of life. One of my greatest passions is to inspire people to want more of God. To pursue *more* of his purpose and plan and to dream big God-sized dreams.

## THE INDESCRIBABLE GOD

What would you answer if I asked you to complete this sentence: "God is ..."? Most people would answer with something they'd already discovered about God: God is my peace, God is righteous, God is my healer, God is my protector, God is all-knowing, God is my provider. While all of those would be right answers, those adjectives and nouns and a thousand more still would not define God, because God is more than we could ever grasp, let alone define.

Even if you said, "God is faithful," he is more faithful than you could possibly imagine. If you said, "God is loving," because you've experienced that love, you still haven't come close to comprehending how abundant that love is.

God is not what he *has been*, nor is he what he *currently is*; God is what he *could be*. In other words, God is more. He certainly is all that you've discovered, but he is also more than you or I could ever dream or imagine.

In the apostle Paul's letter to the church at Ephesus, he writes that God "is able to do immeasurably more than all we ask or imagine" (Eph. 3:20). So if God is indeed more, what keeps us in a state of comfort and complacency? What barriers keep us from experiencing his all?

## THAT TREE'S ON FIRE!

Some of us don't go after more of God because we're afraid of where it might lead. That was my story. Although I grew up in church, I was afraid of what might happen if I opened myself up to whatever God had for me. The possibilities seemed incredibly dangerous. I thought that if I really sold out to God, I'd spend the rest of my life as a missionary living in a mud hut out in the bush. Or that I'd be required to go door to door and warn people to turn from their wickedness or burn in hell. If that was what it meant to experience God's more, I didn't want it. I wanted just enough God to get to heaven, but nothing more.

If you've felt the same way, you're in good company. Even Moses—one of God's great servants—wondered if he really wanted all that God had for him. You know the backstory: a Hebrew baby who was hidden in a basket on the river, found by Pharaoh's family, spared from murder, raised in a palace, and groomed to be prince of Egypt. At age forty, he was exiled from that country and spent forty years in the desert. You could say he was not living out his passion, dreams, and potential. But God wanted to do some incredible things in this guy's life. He had more in store for Moses. So God showed up in a burning bush.

Maybe you've seen the movie in which this bush is engulfed in flames but somehow never burns up. Moses is curious, naturally, so he goes over to check out this burning bush and he hears God calling from within the flames: "Moses! Moses!" When Moses answers, God tells him not to come any closer: "Take off your sandals, for the place where you are standing is holy ground" (Exod. 3:5).

Not your everyday experience, but so many times when God has something big for us, it starts with something we don't understand. If I heard a blazing bush call my name, I'm pretty sure I'd think, *You know what? I'll pretend I never heard that. I think I'm going to leave that one alone.* Can you even imagine Moses trying to explain what happened?

"Hey guys, you'll never guess what I saw today!"

"So tell us about it."

"Well, there was a bush and it was burning—but you know, it really wasn't burning; it was only on fire. And when I went over to take a look, it talked to me. It knew my name! Oh, and guess who the bush was? It was God!"

At that point they'd all be backing away, very slowly. I'm not sure what they would have called it in those days, but in modern terms, we'd think, *That guy's got some serious issues!*

Maybe you've never seen a tree on fire that isn't really burning, but a lot of times, we see things that come across as strange, and our reaction is the same: we back away. Maybe God put someone in your life who seems really odd or needy and you back away. Maybe someone at church asks you to lay hands on him and pray for his healing, but you've never done anything like that, so you come up with an excuse.

Maybe those are your burning bushes that would give you more of what God wants for you.

We're more comfortable with the God who talks to us from a book, or on a video screen at church. These encounters with God are predictable and safe. But beyond our narrow comfort zones, God has more. He has more because he *is* more. He is the God of more than you've ever experienced or imagined. There are scores of believers who will go to heaven but will never experience firsthand all that God prepared for them on earth. When we see that tree on fire, we turn and run.

## LITTLE OLD ME?

In Exodus 3:11, Moses said to God, "Who am I, that I should go to Pharaoh and bring the Israelites out of Egypt?" God answered, "I will be with you. And this will be the sign to you that it is I who have sent you: When you have brought the people out of Egypt, you will worship God on this mountain."

God had something truly big for Moses, but he simply couldn't picture himself doing it. His imagination was limited by his lack of confidence in himself. What he missed at first is what a lot of us miss when God offers us more — God won't ask you to do anything that he won't equip you to do. On your own, you probably can't accomplish what God wants you to do, but you won't be alone. Like Moses, we back away from the more God has for us by asking, "Who am I to be able to undertake this huge challenge?" So many times we are our own biggest barriers from getting God's best. We believe that we first have to get our act together before we can experience the greatness God has for us, when the reverse is true. God wants you just the way you are and will help you get your act together as you answer his call. Most of our heroes in the Bible were untrained and deeply flawed, but God used them anyway.

What adventure are you missing by thinking, *Who am I to try something that big?*

## I DON'T EVEN KNOW YOUR NAME

Moses eventually got past his inferiority complex, but he came up with another excuse for backing away from the big adventure God had for him. He knew that when he went back to the Israelites to try to lead them they would ask who gave him the authority to do that. Moses basically said, "Here's the problem, God. These people are going to ask me who sent me. They're going to ask me your name. So if you don't mind, just tell me what that is." And God says, "No problem. Tell them my name is I AM." If it wasn't so serious, it would be funny—almost like that "Who's on First?" comedy routine:

"So who are you again?"

"I am."

"That's what I'm asking."

But this was God's way of saying he is more than any name a human could understand. We cannot define God with any one word, or with all the words ever written. God will never fit into the tiny box of our intellect, experiences, or imagination. If God always has to fit everything into our understanding, if he always has to fit into our limited human minds, then he will always be less. He will be a very small god whom we can handle, a very safe god who never disrupts our lives. Many times the reason we experience so little of God is that we do not know who he really is. We want to define him, but we don't really want to know him.

## BUT WHAT IF?

Thankfully, Moses didn't give up. But he still wasn't sure he was up to the adventure God had for him. Have you ever been "almost there" with God? You sense that he has something big he wants you to do and you're beginning to run out of excuses, but instead of just jumping in with both feet, you come up with another reason for backing away. That's where Moses was when he asked, "What if they do not believe me or listen to me and say, 'the LORD did not appear to you'?" (4:1). In a sense he was saying, "Okay, God, I understand I don't have to do this on my own, and I now realize just how big and mighty you are. I'm leaning your way, but what if they laugh at me? What if they make fun of me? What if they think I'm crazy?"

I've learned over the years that it's the "what ifs" that often hold people back from experiencing the more of God. It's why we're content to go to church every Sunday, listen to the sermon, maybe raise our hands in worship, then go back to our daily routines. You might have been challenged by the sermon to step out and volunteer at an urban ministry, but you thought, *What if my friends think I'm nuts?* You might have sensed God calling you to share your faith journey with a colleague at work, but you thought, *What if I offend her?*

God answered Moses with a question: "What is that in your hand?" To Moses, it was a simple staff, basically a walking stick. But by the time God was finished with it, it had become a snake. God was saying to Moses, "Trust me and I can do wonders that will validate you and draw others to you for my sake." Once again he reassures us that it's not up to us. We come to him with little, and he transforms it into something phenomenal.

This was also God's way of saying to Moses, "Get over your fear of what others think! If I can turn a piece of wood into a snake, why are you so worried about what people think of you?" I can pretty much guarantee you that whenever you obey God when he asks you to step out of your comfort zone, there will always be someone trying to rein you in back to *their* reality. Even your well-meaning Christian friends might try to talk you out of whatever it is God is calling you to do:

> "You know, it's pretty dangerous in that neighborhood."
> "You need to be careful about what you say at work."
> "How are you ever going to pay for it?"
> "*I* understand what you're doing, but *they* might think you're nuts."

If we're going to worry about what others think, we'll simply never get more of God.

I'll never forget the first time I went into a vibrant, lively church service. Having been raised in a very formal church, I'd never experienced a worship service quite like that one. It's probably pretty familiar to you, but it wasn't to me: drums on the stage, some hands clapping, other hands raised, bodies swaying to the upbeat music. Not exactly my idea of church.

The truth is, part of me wasn't sure if this was even right, but another part of me sort of liked it. At first, I fought the desire to join in, but then I timidly tapped my foot a little, and after a couple of

Sundays of nervously looking around to see if others were watching me as I eventually graduated to clapping my hands and even raising my hands slightly above my waist, I finally jumped right in and experienced a freedom in worship I'd never known before.

Why did it take me so long? Why was I worried about what others might think? My "what if" kept me from getting more out of worship, more from God. This isn't an endorsement of any particular style of worship, by the way. I believe God loves our earnest and heartfelt worship regardless of the style. But whenever we hesitate to experience God because we're worried about what others will think, we miss out on the more he wants for us.

We serve a God who is a whole lot more than anything we can understand. That's why it's critical that we have this driving passion and this plan—this spiritual bucket list—to go after more of God. But first we must get past one last excuse.

## I'VE NEVER DONE THAT BEFORE

After seeing his walking stick writhing on the ground, you would think Moses was ready to lead the Israelites into God's great adventure, but instead, he found one last excuse: I've never been very good at speaking in front of large crowds. It's the old "I've never done that before" excuse that I hear so often:

> "I've never been out of the country before, so there's no way I could go on that missions trip."
> "I've never been very good with words and could never tell my story in front of the entire church."
> "I've never done anything like that, so why start now?"

It's at this point that God got angry with Moses and got in his face a little. He told Moses that his brother, Aaron, could serve as his spokesman if he was too afraid of doing it himself, but then he added these words that all of us need to grab hold of whenever we start making excuses to God: I will help you and I will teach you (4:15).

Just as God wanted to do things through Moses that stretched far beyond what he could have ever dreamed, he invites each of us into similar adventures. We can continue to make excuses until God moves on to accomplish his purposes with someone else. Or we can take whatever it is we have in our hands and let God use it for his kingdom. He desires to let us share in the adventure, to experience things so amazing that we never want to go back to the safe and predictable lives we once led.

Moses took his walking stick and found Aaron and told him everything that God had said to him. Together, they went to the Israelites and repeated what they had heard from God. When the people heard just how much God cared about them, they bowed down and worshiped.

All because Moses finally believed that God was more than he could ever imagine.

I'll admit that checking everything off on my bucket list is a pretty big stretch. But that's not going to stop me from trying. I also know that God has some things on his bucket list for me that will seem even more daunting. If I never get to fly an F-16, it won't be the end of the world. What I never want to miss, however, is a chance to join God on whatever adventure he has for me. I don't know what that will be for me, or for you.

All I know for sure is that it will be more than either of us could ever imagine. Because God is more.

# CHAPTER 17

# G O D
## IS FATHER

*Craig Groeschel*

I think I'm a pretty decent father, and here's why: I hate cats. I am not cruel to cats; I simply don't like them. Having said that, our family has a cat. Does that make me a hypocrite? No. It makes me a pretty good dad because the only reason we have a cat is because I love my kids. They love cats, so I let them have one.

She is a female outdoor cat. Unfortunately, because we put off getting her fixed, we suddenly found ourselves with seven cats — our cat plus her six kittens — right around Father's Day. While it might be appropriate to honor their father for Father's Day, we don't know who the father is, which tells you something about the morals of this cat.

When the kittens came, my children begged me to let them keep them. I have six children, so that would mean each child could technically have his or her very own illegitimate feline pet. I don't want my children to grow up believing that kind of loose behavior is acceptable in our home, so we gave them all away to good homes. (The kittens, not the children.)

I share this story because I'd like you to think I am a pretty good father. Most dads think they're also "pretty good," but in all honesty, we wish we could be much better. Fortunately, we have someone we can look up to: our heavenly Father. God has many roles in the lives of a Christ follower, but perhaps the most comforting is his role as father.

Isaiah 64:8 says, "Yet, O LORD, you are our Father. We are the clay, you are the potter; we are all the work of your hand." In Matthew 6:9, Jesus was teaching his disciples how to pray. He said this is how you begin: "Our Father in heaven, hallowed be your name." In fact, when Jesus talked to his heavenly Father, he called him by one of the most intimate phrases in Aramaic, the language Jesus spoke: *Abba*. Abba literally means "Daddy" or "Papa." One of the very first words that babies learn to say, regardless of culture, language, or nationality, is *dada, papa*, or *abba*. It's as if every infant child on the planet seeks to express their innate need for a father.

God is Father.

## A GREAT DADDY

I have six children, but I can remember the first time each one said, "Da-da!" My heart melted every time. (Honestly, it still does.) If you're a mother, you probably remember the same thing: "Ma-ma." These words express an intimacy that immediately draws your heart in. That is the level of intimacy that God invites us to enjoy with him, to be able to call out to him, "Daddy!"

When my kids were very little, I used to train them. I'd say, "Who's the greatest of them all?" And they would shout, "Dada! Dada!" I know that's shameless self-promotion, but it's what we dads have to do to feel good about ourselves. That, and let our kids have animals that we hate. It works, most of the time. One day I was feeling the need for some affirmation, so I again asked, "Who's the greatest of them all?" One of my kids answered, "Mama!" They all thought that was hilarious, so now that's all they'll answer if I ask that question.

When he was eight years old, I remember asking my oldest boy, Sam, "Hey buddy, what do you want to be when you grow up?" I'll never forget his answer. He opened his eyes wide and smiled and said, "I want to be what you are, Daddy." I remember thinking, *Wow. That's so cool.* I said, "So you want to be a preacher, just like me?" He giggled and said, "No, Daddy! I want to be what you are — I want to be a great daddy." That would have been the perfect moment for Sam to ask for a pony or a sports car or something. I would have given him anything. If he still says that when he's eighteen or thirty-eight, then I'll know I've done something right. What better compliment could a child pay their father?

"I want to be like you — I want to be a great daddy."

The greatest daddy who's ever lived is Abba God, our heavenly Father. Maybe you had a great father. Or maybe you'd say your dad wasn't quite as involved as you would have liked. Maybe he felt distant, disengaged. Whether you had the best father or one who disappointed you, your earthly father was nothing like your heavenly Father. Our heavenly Father is simply the greatest father who ever lived. He's the standard for all fathers universally. To illustrate just how great a father we have in God, Jesus told a familiar story that we commonly refer to as the story of the prodigal son. In your Bible, this section might be titled "The Prodigal Son" or "The Parable of the Lost Son." I don't think either of these titles is accurate, though, because it's a story about *two* sons, and both are important. However, the most important player in this story is not either of the two sons but the father. This father represents our heavenly Father, and it's his actions, his responses, that describe the kind of father he is to each of us.

The story begins with the younger son asking his dad for his share of the inheritance. Essentially this son said, "I want my money now. I'm getting out of here. I'm tired of your rules. I want to do my life on my own." Dad gave him the money and he took off, and soon after, he was broke, due to what the Bible called "wild living." Practically overnight this son blew through his entire inheritance.

Not only that, but a severe famine struck the country, which really put him in bad shape, so he decided to return to his father's place and offer to work as a servant, because he felt unworthy to be treated as a son. As he approached his home, his father saw him, ran to him, and kissed him. Here's how the Bible records his return: "The son said to him, 'Father, I have sinned against heaven and against you. I am no longer worthy to be called your son.' But the father said to his servants, 'Quick! Bring the best robe and put it on him. Put a ring on his finger and sandals on his feet. Bring the fattened calf and kill it. Let's have a feast and celebrate. For this son of mine was dead and is alive again; he was lost and is found.' So they began to celebrate" (Luke 15:21 – 24).

When I was a kid, I idolized my dad. Eventually, of course, I realized that my dad is human. But before that time, I would tell all my friends, "My dad can beat up your dad." And I honestly believed that he could. To this day, I still think he can. He's close to seventy, but I still think he could whip me; he just has that old man "something." But I really would brag to my friends that my dad was tough. Not once did I ever say, "My dad's more sensitive than your dad!" Guys just don't do that. As sons, we like to see our fathers as strong and invincible.

Most of us get the fact that God is powerful. But this story beautifully illustrates a softer side of our heavenly Father. A father who loves us unconditionally. A father who runs toward us even after we have turned our backs on him.

## A PATIENT FATHER

If you're a parent, you know how difficult it can be to wait for your children to come around and do the right thing. But that's exactly what the father did in this story that Jesus told. He waited. And waited. And waited. And waited some more. He probably heard bad reports about things his son was into. If that story was set in this century, he probably would have heard rumors like these: "Your son wrecked his car," "He's smoking weed," "He runs around with loose women," "He's at frat parties," "He's running up debt," "He robbed a liquor store." Can you imagine being a dad and hearing things like that?

Unlike most of us regular dads, our heavenly Father is patient, not just for the sake of being patient but because he wants to give you as much time as you need to come to your senses. He isn't waiting for you to mess up so that he can punish you; he waits so that you can experience his forgiveness: "He is patient with you, not wanting anyone to perish, but everyone to come to repentance" (2 Peter 3:9).

Here's what the father *didn't* do: he loved his son enough not to interrupt his downward, purposeful spiral. Probably everything in him wanted to intervene. He likely wanted to come to his rescue, especially if he heard his son was going hungry. "Hey, I know I gave you what was yours, but here's a little more. It's ridiculous for you to be working at a pig farm. Please come home." But his father loved him enough to wait.

I can almost picture him standing at the edge of town every day, gazing off into the distance: "I wonder if today is going to be the day. I wonder if today he's going to come to his senses and come home. I wonder if today is the day when he realizes that a bad day at my house is better than a good day in his sin. Will it be today?" Every day he strains with his hand over his eyes: "Is that him in the distance?"

God the Father is still waiting for those who have not yet come home, which ought to give you great comfort if you have a family member or loved one who is far from God. Maybe today they will hear his voice calling out to them. You never want to see someone hit bottom like the prodigal son did, but maybe that's what it will take for a wayward son or daughter to hear God's tender voice inviting them to come home. I know people whom I'm very close to who took their metaphorical inheritance and ran, and I'm so thankful that God doesn't give up on them, that he is waiting patiently for their return.

You might be tempted to think that some have wandered too far and have sinned so greatly that there's no hope for them, but with God, there is always hope. No one is outside the boundaries of his love. Consider the story of the apostle Paul, who earned a reputation for tracking down Christians and murdering them—a hardcore sinner if there ever was one. Yet at just the right moment, God met him and gave him the ultimate second chance. Why? God's ways are always perfect: "But for that very reason I was shown mercy so that in me, the worst of sinners, Christ Jesus might display his unlimited patience as an example for those who would believe on him and receive eternal life" (1 Tim. 1:16). If God was willing to wait for Paul, who singled out Christians and murdered them, don't you think he's willing to wait for that person for whom you've been praying? God is patient. He never gives up on people, and we shouldn't either.

# A FORGIVING FATHER

God is a patient father because he wants to give his children something they don't deserve: forgiveness: "In him we have redemption through his blood, the forgiveness of sins, in accordance with the riches of God's grace that he lavished on us with all wisdom and understanding" (Eph. 1:7–8).

There's a human tendency, not just in fathers, to hear stories of someone who has gotten into some real trouble and ended up paying dearly for it and think, *Well, he got exactly what he deserved.* This wayward son who disrespected his father and trashed the family name probably deserved to be left in the pig pen. I'd *like* to think I would eventually forgive a son like that, but I'd probably want to make sure he knew he was getting what he deserved: "See, that's what happens when you go out drinking every night and wasting your money on prostitutes." I might even want him to earn back my love by putting him on a tight leash and giving him a list of things to do to show me he was serious about turning his life around.

A lot of times our forgiveness is conditional, but our heavenly Father offers his forgiveness instantly and without condition. What did the prodigal son have to do to earn his father's forgiveness? Nothing. Not a single thing. According to Scripture, he simply came to his senses one day and went home. He didn't work for it. He didn't make it up to his father. He *did* say he "wasn't worthy," but he never actually apologized. Before he even finished his prepared speech, his father sprang into action to forgive him. The father took off his robe and wrapped it around his filthy son, symbolizing, "I can no longer see the shame and the sin of your guilt. Now I see only my robe, and you look clean." He instructed his servants to prepare a fattened calf, a symbol of sacrifice for forgiveness. And then, they party. Everything's not just okay between them; it's better. My son has returned, and he is completely, totally forgiven.

I read a story once about a father who was facing a serious challenge with his seventeen-year-old son's behavior. Generally, the son was a good kid, but he had one glaring flaw: he constantly disrespected his mother. The dad took him aside one day and explained, "Look, son, you need to understand this: disrespecting your mother stops now. If you do it again—I don't care how big you are—I'm going to treat you like you were six. My belt's coming off, I'm going to turn you over, and you're going to get ten licks on your backside. They're going to count, and you're not going to forget them. You are not to disrespect your mother, ever again."

You can probably guess what happened. The teenager disrespected his mother one more time. The dad dropped what he was doing and said, "That's enough! Come over here. These are going to be ten licks so hard you're never going to forget them."

He removed his belt and then stood, frozen for a moment, deep in thought. Suddenly, he handed the belt to his son. His son just stood there, startled, the belt dangling from his hand. His father said, "You know what? Here's what we're going to do. You're going to whip me. The punishment has to stand. But I love you. So I'm going to take the punishment for you." He spread his hands and leaned forward, placing them on the wall. He drew a deep breath, braced himself, and told his son, "Hit me. As hard as you can. Ten times."

His son protested, "I can't do that!"

The dad insisted. "No! That's the punishment. And it stands. Now hit me."

The son halfheartedly smacked his dad.

The dad turned and grabbed his son by the hands, holding them together, still clutching the belt. "No! That one doesn't count. It's ten times, as hard as you can."

He turned back to the wall and braced himself again. Through tears, the son lashed out, striking his father time after time after time. His father clenched his teeth and accepted the punishment in his child's place.

God did exactly the same for us. He became one of us in the person of his Son, Jesus. Jesus became sin for us on the cross, shed his blood, and rose again. So now, when you hear about the forgiveness of your sins, you should understand what it cost God the Father: his only Son. Our God desires so much to forgive us of all our filth that he was willing to take the punishment for us. He is a forgiving father.

In Isaiah 43:25, God says, "I, even I, am he who blots out your transgressions, for my own sake, and remembers your sins no more."

He deliberately forgets your confessed sins. There's nothing God cannot do. One thing he *chooses* not to do is to remember your sins—when they are covered under Jesus' blood. That's the kind of father he is. He is waiting patiently for you, forgiveness in his eyes and in his arms.

# A PROUD FATHER

I love what the prodigal's father did when he saw his wayward son from afar off: he ran. You have to realize, in Jesus' day, men wore robes. A man's robe would have a slit down the side, so that he could work and not be hindered. Because of the slit, a man would never run or even jog in his robe because if he did, he would expose his leg. According to Jewish law, exposing that part of your body—your upper thigh—was downright shameful. But this loving, patient, forgiving, intimate father didn't care. I know that pride is one of the seven deadly sins, but I know something about being a dad, and as far as I'm concerned, this was one proud father who couldn't have cared less that he was making himself look foolish.

No matter what we do, our heavenly Father is proud of us.

My second daughter, Mandy, is an exceptional speller. Not only can she can spell words that I can't, but she can spell words that I wouldn't even know how to look up. Mandy recently won a regional spelling bee, which meant she got to compete in the state spelling championship. This was not her first regional win, either. Every time we go to one of these things, all of us parents are probably more nervous than our kids.

At the state competition, about sixty kids faced off. Whenever it was Mandy's turn to spell a word, my wife, Amy, and I were on pins and needles. After she spelled the word, I would immediately look to the judge to see if she got it right. She did! Eventually, the field would narrow and Mandy was in the top forty. Then the top thirty. Then the top twenty. It seemed to go on forever; these kids were great and kept spelling long and unfamiliar words correctly. Suddenly, only three kids remained, and Mandy was one of them.

The first kid was given a word and spelled it incorrectly. The second one was given a word and she too missed it. Only one word stood between Mandy and the state championship, which would also mean a trip to the national spelling bee in Washington, D.C. It took all the discipline I could muster, telling myself, *When she wins, don't cheer, don't shout. Don't embarrass her. Don't jump up, don't stand on the table. Do not do* anything *that will make her hate you for the rest of your life.*

Mandy took the stage, listened to the word, and spelled it ... incorrectly.

They had a runoff between those three finalists, and one of the other students won the spelling bee. Of course, Mandy was disappointed. One of the prizes that Mandy really hoped to win was a video iPod. Do you know how much those things cost? Those who know me know that no child of mine will ever get a $250 video iPod. But I was so proud of her for even making it to regionals, let alone being in the top three. On the drive home, I pretended I needed to run an errand. I went into a big box store, charged straight to the counter, and said, "One video iPod, please." I didn't even look at the price. When I got back to the car, I took it out of the sack and handed it to Mandy.

I wanted her to know that no matter how she performed, I was proud of her.

God is not just proud of you; he's crazy about you. He loves you whether you come in first at the spelling bee or dead last. You don't have to earn his admiration with your performance. Everyone else might think you're a loser, but to God, you're a beautiful winner; he's proud of you just because of who you are.

I hope you had a father who was patient with you, but chances are you tested his patience to the limit and experienced his anger and frustration. I also hope you had a father who was quick to forgive, but I know how easy it is for dads to bypass forgiveness on the way to punishment. And I would love to think that your father let you know how proud he was of you. He probably was, but dads don't always show it.

But regardless of what kind of father you had as a child, you have a perfect heavenly Father who will always be there when you fall, lifting you into his warm embrace as you look into his forgiving eyes and exclaim, "Oh thank you, Daddy! You're the best father I could ever have!"

# CONTRIBUTORS

**Mark Batterson** has been the lead pastor of National Community Church in Washington, D. C., since January 7, 1996, when he started the church with three members: himself, his wife, and his son. Today, National Community Church serves two thousand people every weekend in eight services at four locations in and around the district.

Mark never really intended to become a pastor, but as a young man attending the University of Chicago on a basketball scholarship, he asked God, "What do you want me to do with my life?" He sensed God wanted him to plant a church, so he left the university in favor of Central Bible College to prepare for ministry. While in seminary at Trinity Evangelical Divinity School, he planted a church that failed.

His second attempt was National Community Church, named one of the twenty-five most innovative churches in America and one of the fifty most influential churches—both by *Outreach* magazine. Approximately seventy percent of its adherents are single twentysomethings. Believing that they are "called to the marketplace," the congregation of NCC meets in movie theaters and Metro stops throughout the D.C. area. The only building the church owns is the largest coffeehouse on Capitol Hill, serving approximately five hundred customers daily. All profit from the coffeehouse goes to the nearly one-hundred missionaries and international ministries the church supports.

Mark is the author of *In a Pit with a Lion on a Snowy Day*, *Wild Goose Chase*, and *Primal: A Quest for the Lost Soul of Christianity*. He is married to Lora, and they have three children, Parker, Summer, and Josiah.

**Rick Bezet** is the founder and lead pastor of New Life Church (*http://www.newlifechurch.tv/*) in central Arkansas. A former professional golfer, Rick set aside his future to follow God's call and move his family to Conway, Arkansas, to start New Life in 2001. He established the church to attract the unchurched and "dechurched" of the region, knowing that many people have been hurt by previous church experiences. By combining cultural relevancy with pure doctrine, New Life has grown rapidly into four campuses that provide eleven weekend services. They will soon launch the Arkansas Dream Center, an outreach ministry in downtown Little Rock.

Rick also is one of the founding pastors of the Association of Related Churches (ARC), an organization designed to plant churches and impact the world through missions. Their goal in 2009 was to plant fifty churches, the equivalent of a new plant every seven days.

Rick and his wife, Michelle, have four children: Hunter, Hailee, Tanner, and Grace. In his spare time, Rick likes to golf and watch the Louisiana State University Tigers.

**John Burke** is the lead pastor at Gateway Community Church (*http://www.gatewaychurch.com/*) in Austin, Texas. In 1998 John, his wife, Kathy, and ten others who had been meeting in a home started Gateway "to reach the post-Christian, postmodern culture" of their city. The majority of people at Gateway were not Christ followers before coming. Seventy-five percent are under forty, and half are single. There are currently more than four thousand people who attend each weekend at one of the two locations. Gateway Church is all about helping unchurched people become a unified community of growing, multiplying Christ followers (Matt. 28:18–20; Eph. 4:12–13). According to John, "Jesus never saw church as a place to go but as a people who love him and who are learning to love others." Gateway is a place where God meets seeking people who are far from perfect. Their message is "Come as you are, no matter what your spiritual background or past or where you are now." Anyone is welcome. But they also say, "But don't stay that way." Their desire is that each person becomes who God intended them to be as they walk together in community.

John is the author of *No Perfect People Allowed* and *Soul Revolution: How Imperfect People Become All God Intended* (*www.soul-*

*revolution.net*). He is also the president of Emerging Leadership Initiative (ELI), a nonprofit organization founded to help establish a multiplying network of missional churches that envision, equip, and empower young emerging leaders to raise the church up out of the culture while maintaining biblical integrity. Before starting Gateway, John was the executive director of ministries at Willow Creek Community Church. He and Kathy are the parents of two children, Ashley and Justin.

**Francis Chan** is the pastor of Cornerstone Church (*http://www .cornerstonesimi.com/*) in Simi Valley, California, where he has been serving for the past fifteen years. To serve its growing and diverse congregation, Cornerstone has developed four neighborhood-based "communities" and has also planted ten churches in California, Oregon, Ohio, Texas, and Colorado. Francis also is the founder and chancellor of Eternity Bible College and serves on the board of directors for Children's Hunger Fund and World Impact.

Because of his passion to see the next generation of American Christians display a much deeper love for Jesus and their neighbors, Francis spends much of his time speaking to high school and college students. An accomplished writer, he is the author of *Crazy Love* and *Forgotten God*. Francis is married to Lisa, and they have three daughters and one son.

**Wayne Cordeiro** is the founding pastor of New Hope Christian Fellowship (*http://www.enewhope.org/*) in Honolulu, Hawaii. One of the nation's fastest growing churches with more than fourteen thousand in weekend attendance, New Hope is also listed as one of the top ten most innovative churches in America, with more than three thousand people attending services each week via the internet. New Hope has seen more than fifty-three thousand first-time decisions in Hawaii since its inception twenty-six years ago.

Wayne is a church planter at heart, with more than 105 churches planted in the Pacific Rim and beyond, including Hawaii, Seattle, Los Angeles, Las Vegas, the Philippines, Japan, Australia, and Myanmar. He is also a trainer of leaders as chancellor of the consortium of Pacific Rim Christian Colleges, with locations in Hawaii,

Oregon, Myanmar, and Tokyo training emerging leaders from around the world.

Wayne is the author of nine books, including *Doing Church as a Team, Dream Releasers, The Seven Rules of Success, The Divine Mentor, Leading On Empty,* and *The Encore Church.*

Wayne and his wife, Anna, have three married children and three grandchildren. His hobbies include music, reading, water sports, and riding his Harley Davidson, but most of all, spending time with his grandchildren.

**Jentezen Franklin** was serving as an evangelist when he was asked to preach at Free Chapel (*http://www.freechapel.org*) in Gainesville, Georgia. It turns out that he ended up preaching at the funeral of the church's pastor, who had died suddenly. Following the funeral, he was asked to become the pastor of the church, and he has served in that capacity ever since.

In his twenty years at Free Chapel he has seen the church grow to a congregation of 12,400, with an additional congregation in Irvine, California, of two thousand. The Georgia church occupies a 160,000 square foot facility on 154 acres, while the California campus is an 88,000 square foot converted office building in the heart of the Irvine business district.

Jentezen grew up as a pastor's kid and credits both his parents with showing him how to seek God through the study of the Bible, prayer, and fasting. His interest in the latter led him to write a book, *Fasting,* which became a *New York Times* bestseller, and which began a "fasting movement" joined by hundreds of thousands of people around the world. "The act of fasting retrains us away from dependence on the satisfaction of our desires and makes the kingdom of God our primary focus in our daily lives," Jentezen says.

What motivates both Jentezen and his church can be summed up in a single word: souls. "In everything we do—whether an illustrated sermon or a special program—our main focus is, 'How can we use this to reach souls?'" Jentezen explains. "We are serious about the salvation of souls."

Jentezen is a graduate of Atlantic Christian College (now Barton College) in Wilson, North Carolina. He is married to Cherise, and they have five children.

**Steven Furtick** is the founding pastor of Elevation Church (*http://www.elevationchurch.org/*) in Charlotte, North Carolina, which has been named one of the "Ten Fastest Growing Churches in America" by *Outreach* magazine.

The heart of Steven's message is revolutionary faith and how to approach every experience from a visionary perspective. As a leader under thirty years old, his unique passion for seeing God's purposes fulfilled is igniting a fire in Charlotte and beyond.

Steven attended North Greenville University, received a BA in communications, and went on to complete a Master of Divinity from Southern Baptist Theological Seminary.

He resides in the Charlotte area with his wife, Holly, and two sons, Elijah and Graham.

**Craig Groeschel** is the founding pastor of Lifechurch.tv (*http://www.lifechurch.tv/*), which operates thirteen campuses in five states. *Outreach* magazine named Lifechurch.tv the most innovative and second largest church in the United States. In addition to the twenty-six thousand people who attend Lifechurch.tv, another hundred thousand people from 150 countries are reached weekly through its online campus, the first of its kind.

Passionate about presenting "the uncompromised gospel in a way that people can understand," Craig started YouVersion, a free Bible that has been given away to 2.5 million people for use on their cell phones. He also provides free ministry-related materials to other churches. More than thirty-five thousand churches download more than 1 million free ministry products annually.

In addition to serving as the compiler for this book, Craig has written five books, including *The Christian Atheist*, *It*, and *Confessions of a Pastor*. He is married to Amy, and they have four daughters and two sons.

**Chris Hodges** is the founding and senior pastor of Church of the Highlands (*http://www.churchofthehighlands.com/welcome.html*), which began in Birmingham, Alabama. While in Birmingham to attend the SEC baseball tournament, Chris visited a local Barnes and Noble and looked out over the balcony of the bookstore onto the city below. At that moment he knew that God was calling him to start a church that would engage people and allow them to "reach higher heights." From that first official Sunday on February 4, 2001, the church has continued to grow: from a friend's living room to an office complex to a high school auditorium. Named the fastest growing church in the nation in 2008 by *Outreach* magazine, Highlands is now averaging thirteen thousand attendees among six campuses throughout Alabama. The church recently opened the Birmingham Dream Center, which is intended to give them greater opportunities to offer hope and help to the city. Chris and his wife, Tammy, have five children and live in Birmingham.

**Clark Mitchell** is the founder and senior pastor of Journey Church (*http://www.journeychurch.cc/*) in Norman, Oklahoma, with more than twenty years of ministry experience. Building upon Ephesians 3:20 (MSG), "God can do anything, you know—far more than you could ever imagine or guess or request in your wildest dreams! He does it not by pushing us around but by working within in us, his Spirit deeply and gently within us," Journey Church was founded in 2001 with a gathering of thirty-five and has grown to a weekend experience with forty-five hundred in attendance.

Clark is known for his creative teaching style focused on helping people live into their God-given potential and dreams. Journey continues to strive to see a city transformed, one life at a time, by equipping all ages to live a life of influence through biblical leadership and by helping others break the cycle of poverty in their lives. Most of all, Clark loves speaking into the lives of the thousands of children, youth, and college students who call Journey home.

Clark and his wife, Robin, have been married for nineteen years. They have three children and reside in Norman, Oklahoma.

**Perry Noble** serves as pastor of NewSpring Church (*http://www .newspring.cc/*), which has campuses in the South Carolina cities of Anderson, Columbia, Florence, and Greenville. The campuses at Anderson and Columbia are located in permanent facilities, while Greenville and Florence meet in their towns' convention centers. Approximately eleven thousand people attend NewSpring, which began in January 2000 and is affiliated with the Southern Baptist Convention.

Prior to starting NewSpring, Perry served on staffs at churches in Pickens and Anderson, South Carolina. In 1999 a friend asked him, "What would you be willing to attempt for God if you knew you could not fail?" When he answered that he would start a church, his friend replied, "You're a coward if you don't do it." That convinced him. "I knew it was God's way of leading me to start NewSpring," said Noble.

Perry is the author of *Blueprints*, a book on relationships, and is currently working on his second book. He and his wife of nine years, Lucretia, have a daughter, Charisse.

**Dino Rizzo** is the founding pastor of Healing Place Church (*http://healingplacechurch.org/*) in Baton Rouge, Louisiana, a church with over 7,200 people in eleven campuses and eighteen weekend services. HPC has been named one of America's Top Twenty-five Most Innovative Churches, a reflection of Dino's overwhelming drive to reach the unreachable and to engage with others to show God's love to the poor and hurting, wherever they are. His book, *Servolution*, exposes his passion to see believers join together in a revolution of serving others, Jesus style. Dino and his wife, DeLynn, have three children. Visit his blog at *http://www.dinorizzo.com* to learn more.

**Gary Shiohama** is the founding and senior pastor of South Bay Community Church (*http://www.southbaycommunitychurch.com/*), a growing and ethnically diverse congregation of more than seven hundred people in the South Bay suburb of Los Angeles.

Gary grew up in Los Angeles and attended Pepperdine University, where he became a Christian. After college, his longtime interest in politics led him to accept the position of deputy to the president of the Los Angeles City Council, where he served for nearly eight years. Later he opened a Mexican restaurant and also served for a short time as the spokesman for the oil industry for the western United States. He believes his involvement in the public and private sectors helped prepare him for the challenge of leading a growing congregation.

Gary first sensed a call into ministry during his years in politics, but it wasn't until his restaurant business failed that God got his attention. In 1992, with a driving passion to reach people who are far from God, he planted South Bay Community Church with a team of twenty people. The church, which got its start in a community center, has been meeting for the past ten years in a warehouse owned by Public Storage Pick-up and Delivery. Since its move to the warehouse, the church has transitioned from one to four services. Today, the most formidable challenge facing the church is lack of space. It has outgrown its location and is struggling to find a larger facility in South Bay, where real estate is costly and scarce.

Over the years, the church has evolved from a predominantly Asian-American congregation to one which mirrors its ethnically and culturally diverse community. The people of South Bay Community Church are intentional about reaching the church's surrounding community with the gospel, which reflects Gary's passion for evangelism and discipleship.

Gary is married to Cheryl and has three children, Brandon, Kailie, and Natalie. In his spare time Gary enjoys working out, reading, attending Los Angeles Angels baseball games, and collecting Star Wars action figures.

**Toby Slough** was planning to use his business marketing degree to help him land a sales job and become wealthy. But during his senior year at Abilene Christian University, he felt God's call to go into the ministry. After serving as a youth pastor in San Antonio and Oklahoma City, he, with thirteen families, started Cross Timbers Community Church (*http://dnn.crosstimberschurch.org/*) in the back of a bar. Today, Cross Timbers meets in three Texas towns, Argyle, Keller, and Denton. Average weekly attendance at the three locations totals forty-eight hundred.

Toby's passion is to see "broken, hurting people find freedom and life change through a personal relationship with Jesus Christ." It happens regularly and begins with the church's theme, "Welcome Home." As Toby puts it, "The most gratifying thing I hear new people say when they attend our church is that they feel welcome and accepted." Cross Timbers also attempts to care for the whole person and was featured on CNN in 2009 for its work helping people in financial crisis.

Toby and his wife, Mika, have two children, Bailey and Ross, who are students at Oklahoma State University.

**Andy Stanley** is the senior pastor of North Point Ministries (*http://www.northpoint.org/*) in Alpharetta, Georgia, a suburb of Atlanta. After receiving degrees from Georgia State University and Dallas Theological Seminary, Andy served for several years as an associate pastor and minister to students at First Baptist Atlanta. In 1995, he and five others founded North Point Ministries, which now has three campuses in the Atlanta area (North Point Community Church, Buckhead Church, and Browns Bridge Community Church) and has planted more than fifteen partner churches throughout the United States and Canada. From the beginning, North Point's vision has been to create churches that the unchurched love to attend.

In 2006, Buckhead Church was featured in *USA Today* for its use of high definition video in place of a live speaker at its campus. North Point has also been named one of the nation's most influential churches by *The Church Report*, which also included Andy in its list of the nation's most influential pastors.

Andy is a prolific author. His books include *The Principle of the Path* and *The Next Generation Leader*. In 2009, he was selected to be one of the speakers at the National Prayer Service following the inauguration of President Barak Obama. Andy and his wife, Sandra, have three children, Andrew, Garrett, and Allie.

**Greg Surratt** is the founding pastor of Seacoast Church (*http://www.seacoast.org/*), one of the early adopters of the multisite model. Located in Mt. Pleasant, South Carolina, Seacoast has been recognized by various media as an innovative and influential church that pioneers new strategies for church growth and development. The church combines a unique approach to highly participatory worship with a heart for missional evangelism. Greg describes their weekend services as a "practical, Spirit-filled, but nonspooky, yet kind of mystical worship experience, done in multiple locations, very inexpensively." Seacoast has more than ten thousand people attending twenty-nine weekend worship experiences in thirteen locations.

Greg and his wife, Debbie, have four children and six grandchildren. He enjoys reading, photography, fishing, golfing, and rooting for lost causes: the Cubs, Broncos, and Gamecocks.

**Stovall Weems** is the founding and lead pastor of Celebration Church (*http://www.celebration.org/*) in Jacksonville, Florida. The church has grown from a launch team of seven people in 1998 to a multisite ministry of ten campuses that reach ten thousand people every week. Innovative from the beginning, the church recently pioneered what it calls Extension Gatherings—taking their church to homes, coffeehouses, theaters, prisons, military bases, and anyplace else where community and relationships exist. The church serves more than seventy-five Extension Gatherings nationally and internationally.

Through local, national, and international television, Celebration Church broadcasts its services to more than two hundred countries and is seen in over 60 million homes across the United States. Though unaffiliated with a denomination, Stovall, along with several other pastors, formed the Association of Related Churches and provides leadership to that organization, which is committed to church planting.

# THE CHURCH STANDS TOGETHER
## to SHARE, SERVE, and GIVE.

We pray to Jesus asking Him
to answer our prayers.

## What if we became the answer to His?

In John 17:20-24, He prayed that we would
be one, and One Prayer is a movement to see
what can be accomplished when the Church
works together.

Since 2008, millions of believers around the
world have united to share resources, serve our
communities, and give to a meaningful cause.

See how God has worked through One Prayer
to leave a permanent imprint of Christ on
the world.

**www.oneprayer.com**

# It

## How Churches and Leaders Can Get It and Keep It

*Craig Groeschel*

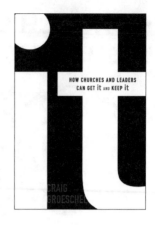

When Craig Groeschel founded LifeChurch.tv, the congregation met in a borrowed two-car garage with ratty furnishings and faulty audiovisual equipment. But people were drawn there, sensing a powerful, life-changing force Groeschel calls *it*.

What is *it*, and how can you and your ministry get—and keep—*it*? Combining in-your-face honesty with off-the-wall humor, this book tells how any believer can obtain *it*, get *it* back, and guard *it*.

One of today's most innovative church leaders, Groeschel provides profile interviews with Mark Driscoll, Perry Noble, Tim Stevens, Mark Batterson, Jud Wilhite, and Dino Rizzo.

This lively book will challenge churches and their leaders to maintain the spiritual balance that results in experiencing *it* in their lives.

**Also available as an eBook and audio download.**

*Available in stores and online!*

# It

## How Churches and Leaders Can Get It and Keep It

*Craig Groeschel*

## DVD

Craig Groeschel, founding and senior
pastor of LifeChurch.tv, takes you on a nine-session video journey to discover the powerful presence from God that he calls *it*
at work in many churches. Each video session is approximately
ten-minutes long and focuses on the many facets of what *it* is
and where *it* comes from. Craig explores the necessary contri-
butions to *it*, such as vision, divine focus, unmistakable camara-
derie, innovative minds, willingness to fall short, hearts focused
outward, and kingdom-mindedness. He concludes the video
experience with a session on whether you have *it* and how to
keep *it* once you have *it*. This video is designed for leadership
groups and church groups and includes discussion questions on
the DVD at the end of each session.

*Available in stores and online!*

# The Christian Atheist

## Believing in God but Living as If He Doesn't Exist

*Craig Groeschel*

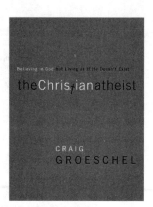

"The more I looked, the more I found Christian Atheists everywhere."

Former Christian Atheist Craig Groeschel knows his subject all too well. After over a decade of successful ministry, he had to make a painful self-admission: although he believed in God, he was leading his church as if God didn't exist.

To Christians and non-Christians alike, to the churched and the unchurched, the journey leading up to Groeschel's admission and the journey that follows—from his family and his upbringing to the lackluster and even diametrically opposed expressions of faith he encountered—will look and sound like the story of their own lives.

Now the founding and senior pastor of the multicampus, pace-setting LiveChurch.tv, Groeschel's personal journey toward a more authentic God-honoring life is more relevant than ever.

Christians and Christian Atheists everywhere will be nodding their heads as they are challenged to take their own honest moment and ask the question: am I putting my whole faith in God but still living as if everything is up to me?

**Also available as an eBook, audio CD, and audio download.**

*Available in stores and online!*

## Share Your Thoughts

**With the Author:** Your comments will be forwarded to the author when you send them to *zauthor@zondervan.com*.

**With Zondervan:** Submit your review of this book by writing to *zreview@zondervan.com*.

## Free Online Resources at
## www.zondervan.com

**Zondervan AuthorTracker:** Be notified whenever your favorite authors publish new books, go on tour, or post an update about what's happening in their lives at www.zondervan.com/authortracker.

**Daily Bible Verses and Devotions:** Enrich your life with daily Bible verses or devotions that help you start every morning focused on God. Visit www.zondervan.com/newsletters.

**Free Email Publications:** Sign up for newsletters on Christian living, academic resources, church ministry, fiction, children's resources, and more. Visit www.zondervan.com/newsletters.

**Zondervan Bible Search:** Find and compare Bible passages in a variety of translations at www.zondervanbiblesearch.com.

**Other Benefits:** Register yourself to receive online benefits like coupons and special offers, or to participate in research.

**ZONDERVAN®**

ZONDERVAN.com/
AUTHORTRACKER
*follow your favorite authors*